HOW TO DESIGN
A LIFE
WORTH
SMILING
ABOUT

HOW TO DESIGN
A LIFE
WORTH
SMILING
ABOUT

=========== ✳ ===========

Developing Success
in Business and in Life

DARRYL DAVIS

New York Chicago San Francisco Athens London Madrid
Mexico City Milan New Delhi Singapore Sydney Toronto

1 2 3 4 5 6 7 8 9 0   DOC/DOC   1 0 9 8 7 6 5 4

ISBN   978-0-07-181986-2
MHID 0-07-181986-X

e-ISBN   978-0-07-181987-9
e-MHID 0-07-181987-8

Library of Congress Cataloging-in-Publication Data
Davis, Darryl (Darryl D.)
    How to design a life worth smiling about : developing success in business and in life / Darryl Davis.
        pages cm
        ISBN 978-0-07-181986-2 (hardback) — ISBN 0-07-181986-X (hbk)
1. Success in business. 2. Success. 3. Career development. I. Title.
    HF5386.D257 2014
    650.1—dc23   2014006540

McGraw-Hill Education books are available at special quantity discounts to use as premiums and sales promotions or for use in corporate training programs. To contact a representative, please visit the Contact Us pages at www.mhprofessional.com.

Illustrations by Steve Pileggi

CONTENTS

ACKNOWLEDGMENTS

To everyone at McGraw-Hill who has worked on this project: Your support and understanding have been incredible. You are truly an extraordinary team of people, employing incredible skills to help authors through the process of writing a book that they can be proud of.

To all of my students who have been so supportive during the journey of writing this book: You truly have been my inspiration. Each day that I sat down to write, I thought of you. Thank you for all your love, caring, and support, and for opening yourselves up to me.

To my Uncle Jack: Thank you for being my prayer warrior. Your dedication to our faith and your unwavering commitment to staying healthy are truly an inspiration to me. I thank you for all your love.

To my Aunt Nancy: You are so full of love and passion for life that you inspire me to be a better person. Thank you for always being there for me, and for being such an important person in my life and to our entire family.

To Erica, thank you for always being such a great mother to our son, and for being so patient with me.

To Stu Kamen, one of my oldest and closest friends, and my secret weapon in writing: Thank you for the invaluable contribution you've made to this book. I know you had to make many sacrifices to meet our deadlines, and I can't thank you enough for all of your hard work and talent.

To my best friend, Steve Harney: They say that if you can count all your true friends on one hand, you're a lucky man. Well, I'd say that I'm the luckiest man in the world because the support and encouragement you've given me are equivalent to those of five people. Through the years, time after time, you have shown me the true meaning of friendship. I can't thank you enough for your commitment to always being there for me—whether it's for guidance, advice, a good laugh, or just an ear to listen. The term *best friend* doesn't adequately describe how important you are to me. And I thank you for being patient with me and helping me discover my calling in life. ☺

To my son, Michael. You are the one who truly puts a smile on my face, especially when I come home from being on the road. You have grown into such a wonderful young man, and I couldn't be prouder of you. I am the luckiest father in the world because of you. There have been so many times when thinking of you, our relationship, and who you are as a human being has inspired me while writing this book. I believe most parents hope that their child will be a better person than themselves, and you have already accomplished that at your young age of 17.

And to the love of my life, April. I cannot adequately express how lucky I feel to have found someone as wonderful as you. My feelings for you are so deep that it would be inappropriate to write in this book what those feelings are, so I will just say this: thank you for your selfless support, your caring about me more than about yourself at times, your abundant love, all you do for our family, and showing me how to live a life worth smiling about. And of course, thank you, honey baby, for all your wonderful contributions to this book. I could not have done this without you. Thank you for helping me make a difference in the world.

Last, but most certainly not least, to my Higher Power, whom I call God. Keep showing me the path you want me to walk, and thank you for never giving up on me.

INTRODUCTION

A Business Book About Smiling—Really?

know what you're thinking. Smiling doesn't seem like a typical topic for a business book. It doesn't seem as important as "leadership" or "goal setting," or even "how to use Microsoft Office." And besides, everyone knows that it's better to smile than to walk around looking angry all day. So, why should I read a 200+ page book to learn what I already know?

Well, frankly, I'd have my doubts, too, if this book were nothing more than a long-winded piece of advice telling you to smile more frequently. Luckily, there's a bit more to it than that.

First of all, what if I told you that smiling more actually *does* help you to succeed? (The first chapter, "The Science Behind Your Smile," goes into that in great detail.) And, what if I further told you that if you know what you truly want in business and in life, get clear about what's stopping you from having what you want, and then take specific actions to get precisely what you want, you'll wind up with more things to smile about? It's kind of obvious, right? And self-fulfilling. (Back to that concept at the end of this introduction.)

As for why you need to read this book in order to take action—well, I suppose you don't really *need* to read it. You could just recognize the obvious and make the appropriate adjustments all on your own. But then again, you already know that you should eat right and exercise properly. Does that mean that you do it? (You should also get enough sleep each day and floss regularly, both of which you already know—but I digress.) The point is, we all need a good kick in the butt every now and then to get us moving down the path that we know we *ought* to be on, when for one reason or another we have gotten stuck. Consider me as the shoe that's providing the kick.

One other concern (or, some may say, objection) that I often get when I present on the subject of designing a life worth smiling about is this: *taking action to increase smiling is like going to a motivational seminar—it feels good at the time, but it never lasts.* I have only one response to this line of thinking, one that the great motivational speaker Zig Ziglar taught me: a lot of things never last—like taking a shower. There are some things that you just have to do over and over in order to continue reaping the full benefit!

And that's all I've got to say about that.

So, let's take a look at what interested me in smiling to begin with.

It's in Our DNA

For more than a quarter century now (that's a substantial period of time, right? I think I just impressed myself!), I've spoken in front of audiences throughout North America, and I can tell you with absolute certainty that people love to laugh. They want to be inspired. They want to be uplifted. They want to share something positive with other people and to genuinely help others to succeed and be happy. Yes, I know that it may not always *seem* this way, what with all the focus on negatives and failure and the constant "gotcha" moments in our 24-hour cable news channels, not to mention reality TV and celebrity gossip magazines and websites. But I know for sure that, at our core, humans are good, kind-hearted, and generous.

Put simply, we are *designed to smile*. In fact, it's in our DNA. Babies in wombs exhibit facial expressions, including blinking, breathing, and smiling. Scientists speculate that this is a reflex, preparing the baby for life "on the outside." And any parent or grandparent knows that one of the most amazing sights is that of a young baby's first real smile after he has come home with you. You may have to wait for six weeks or so, but when it comes—wow! It's the purest expression of joy that you've ever seen. The smile literally takes up the baby's entire face, and, of course, it's impossible for you not to smile back and perpetuate an ongoing "circle of joy" with your infant.

So, if we're literally born ready and rarin' to smile, why aren't we continually happy creatures from day one on? Well, I blame it on the doctor in the hospital at the time of birth. The moment the newborn emerges, *whack!*—she gets smacked on the butt, setting up a pattern of rude awakenings and disappointments from there on out. (Just kidding, Doc, but you get the idea.) The truth is, I believe that we were put on earth with both the capacity and the predisposition to smile. And, if our purpose, so to speak, is to be positive, to smile, and to improve the lives of those around us, then we need to get back to this. We need to live the life that we were meant to live. But, in order to get there, we first have to undo some of the cynicism and negativity that we've adopted in our lives.

Consider this next example of how we've come to limit ourselves.

I'm sure you've heard the expression *anything is possible*. You've seen these words on posters hanging on executives' walls, or maybe in the locker room at your gym. You know the type of poster I'm referring to—with inspirational imagery like a mountain climber at the top of a snowy peak with the sun rising behind him, or a cyclist at the finish line, arms raised in victory. The saying is also a popular Monday morning Facebook status (followed by comments like, "Really? How *possible* is it to get rid of this hangover?"). My point is that we see and hear these words, but they don't sink in because they've become cliché.

Well, I'd like to invite you to examine *anything is possible*. The words are incredibly powerful. Think about them for a moment. When you are open to possibility, your whole perception shifts. Your life becomes exciting; you become energized because you see the world not *as it is*, but as what *it can become*. If you think back to when you were a child, you probably dreamed of endless possibilities. You might have said to your friends, "When I grow up, I'm going to be an astronaut and live on my own planet," or, "I'm going to be the richest person in the world and have my own castle." Whatever you thought about that would make you happy, outrageous as it may have been, you proudly declared it!

I'm pretty sure you *never* said things like, "When I grow up, I'm going to be poor, overweight, and unhappy," or, "I'm going to be tired, cynical, and lonely." So, what happened? How did we go from having endless dreams and hopes, and living from the concept that *anything is possible*, to where we are today?

Now, of course, I'm exaggerating to help illustrate my point. I'm sure that not everyone's life has gone horribly off course. The majority of people probably fall somewhere in the middle, not allowing themselves to dream those big, awesome dreams anymore, but not about to jump off a cliff out of hopelessness either (at least, I hope not). I believe that for most of us, our lives are a big, messy jumble of some areas that are very fulfilling, some areas where we want to move forward in the same general direction we're going but want to improve upon, and some areas that are just not working and that we'd like to cut out altogether. The question is *how do we sort this all out*? How do we get to that place where we have a clear picture of what we want to accomplish and how to get there? How do we bring possibility into reality?

In short, what does a life worth smiling about look like for me, and how can I create it for myself?

Why Am I Writing This Book?

Before I answer those questions, I'd like to give you some background on how I came to write this particular book. I say this because I think that you, as a reader, should know a bit about my background and what inspired me to explore this topic.

I mentioned this earlier, and it bears repeating: I believe that we are born into this world with endless possibilities in front of us and that we're capable of doing more than worrying about ourselves and just surviving. I believe that it's in our nature to want to engage, serve, help, and make a difference in other people's lives. But somehow, along the way, we get away from these fundamental truths. We get caught up in the cycle of dealing with our day-to-day challenges, and we lose sight of our higher purpose.

Let me tell you a bit about the day-to-day challenges that I faced when I was growing up, how they almost derailed me, and how, ultimately, I discovered what I consider to be my higher calling.

In the earlier years of my childhood, my father wasn't around a lot. It wasn't that he didn't love my mother or me, but there were circumstances that often prevented him from being home with us. Because of this, I grew up being very much influenced by my mother. Now, she was a character! She was constantly singing and dancing around the house (seriously). My grandmother had been a Rockette at Radio City Music Hall in New York City, so that was the environment that my mother had been raised in. She had also done some modeling, and her sisters had done some singing; my point here is that there seems to be show business in our blood.

This love of singing and dancing, and a flair for the dramatic, did not escape me. As far back as I can remember I wanted to be an actor. I was in my first play when I was eight. During the next several years, I performed in plays, went on auditions in Manhattan for TV commercials, and took acting classes, including some at the prominent Lee Strasberg Institute. I was crystal clear about my dream of becoming an actor. I was working toward it, and I was happy.

In 1980, when I was 14, my father passed away unexpectedly, and my whole world changed. Now, although he had not been in my life as much as I would have liked, I loved him very much. The death of a parent is difficult enough for a child to deal with, but what made matters much worse was that my mother could not emotionally cope with the loss and had a nervous breakdown. Even in the days immediately following his death, she was not capable of taking care of things. So at the young age of 14, I was forced to step up and take care of the funeral arrangements. I remember picking out the casket, the flowers, and the headstone, along with negotiating payment arrangements with the funeral home. I didn't really question it—I was just going through the motions and attending to the details of what had to be done for my father. Needless to say, this event changed me and the way that I interacted with the world.

When my father passed away, I was attending Maria Regina Catholic High School in Uniondale, New York. After his death, my mother couldn't afford the tuition, so I began my junior year at East Rockaway Public High School. A few months later, only halfway through the school year, my mother informed me that she had met a man whom she was serious about, and she wanted to move to Queens, New York, to be closer to him. This meant that I would have to change schools *again*, move to a new town, and make new friends. I couldn't wrap my brain around this, and I told my mother that I couldn't handle it. Well, she totally understood—*so she moved without me.* Yes, you read that correctly. My mother helped me file papers with the courts to make me an emancipated minor. She moved to Queens, and I stayed behind in East Rockaway. At 16 years old, I was officially an adult—*on paper.* I could legally enter into contracts, sign leases, or do whatever else I needed to do to live on my own. This allowed me to stay and finish high school in East Rockaway and to get my own apartment. I paid the rent by working three, sometimes four, jobs at once, while still going to school.

Now, for the parents reading this, you may wonder how a mother could leave her 16-year-old son to live on his own. Well, I have two things to say about that. The first is that my mother was never the same after my father died. By this time, two years later, I had adjusted to the absence of the nurturing that we usually associate with a mother. I was already taking care of myself; signing the paperwork simply made it official. I really didn't want to move, so I saw this as getting what I wanted— at the time. As for what I think about it now, I choose to think that my mother did the best she could. (There were many years in my adult life when I didn't think that way, however. As you read this book, you'll find a chapter that deals with forgiveness, so hopefully you'll see how I can now say that.)

So, at the age of 16, there was no room for the luxury of living from possibility and dreams; it was all about surviving and paying my bills. As I began to get older and my responsibilities grew, I had to start thinking about a full-time job to support myself.

While I was in college, I heard about real estate sales. It sounded like a great profession: you could be your own boss, make your own hours, and (if you were good at it) earn a nice income. I thought this would be the perfect way to support myself while I pursued acting, so I took an elective course in real estate. After that, I took my licensing course, and finally the state exam (which I passed with flying colors). So there I was: 19 years old, licensed by the state of New York to "facilitate the transfer of real property between a buyer and seller." Yeah, baby! I was feeling very grown up and excited; I was going places!

From the beginning, I seemed to have a natural affinity for the business. I really enjoyed the work, and I was very driven. Success came easily for me right from the start. After a relatively short time, I was asked to become the manager for a new broker in town, and I quickly brought the office to being number one in our marketplace. Things were finally turning around, but the interesting part was what was going on behind the scenes.

As I starting managing and training others, the job became less about me and more about them. I knew in my heart that, as a leader, I was responsible for more than the number of houses these agents sold. I needed to be able to give them guidance, support, and motivation. I understood the qualities that a good leader should have. The problem was *I didn't have them.* You see, while I was experiencing success externally, on the inside I had turned into a pretty angry guy. Being a teenager is confusing enough, even when you have the right support structure and role models around you. Without a father figure, I was struggling to figure out how to be a man. I was selfish, angry, distrustful, and always in "survival mode." The bottom line is that I wasn't the nicest person to be around.

Thankfully, I was able to look at myself and see these weaknesses. I had a love of learning, enjoyed my training as an actor, and always liked to take classes. I decided that it was time to do some work on *me.* Thus I began my own journey of self-improvement. Whatever books there were on finding your "true self," reaching your goals, letting go of your baggage, or all the above, I bought them and read them. If there was a program on being a better person or a better leader, I listened to the cassette tapes (younger people don't know what *those* are!). I attended transformational training programs. I explored my faith and spirituality. I wanted to understand what it means to be human, to find answers to the questions: *Why am I here? What's my purpose in life?*

I had no idea that this journey would prepare me for a whole new career. But as time went on, I realized that my real joy came from helping others—from understanding the internal motivations that make people do (or not do) things that will make them successful. And as I attended other motivational seminars and watched other speakers help people transform their lives, I yearned to do the same.

Helping Others Helps You

That brings us to today. I'm happy to say that 20 years later, I am still living my dream job. I get to fly all over the world to help people have more fun and less stress in their lives, and design a life worth smiling about. I do this by being a professional speaker, trainer, author, and motivator. I work for organizations and associations across many different industries, with a focus on real estate, as you might imagine. I'm really on a mission because, as I mentioned earlier, I believe that we are each born to be happy and fulfilled. But life can throw us curveballs, and we can get thrown off course. As you can imagine from some of what I shared about my personal life, I know what it's like to be thrown curveballs, but manage to get through to the other side.

We have one life with a finite amount of years available to us, and I believe that while we're here, what we all want is to have a loving, nurturing relationship with others (and with ourselves) and to create memorable moments that we can smile about. I believe the answer to that life question of "What's the endgame?" is that we have a life worth smiling about. If you're not happy with who you are or what you're doing in your life, then something's got to change and change now, because our lives are not forever. All we have is right now, today. It's important that in every moment, we are happy with who we are.

Stretch Your Mind

One's mind, once stretched by a new idea, never regains its original dimensions.

—Oliver Wendell Holmes

My commitment in this book is to give you ideas, strategies, and techniques to help you live a more enjoyable life, one that's worth smiling about.

My approach to this is twofold. First, we have to take a look at some things that you may not have seen before—things about who you are and why you do the things you do. You see, chances are, you already have an idea of how to create a life worth smiling about. You probably know that you should be eating healthy foods, managing your finances successfully, and calling your mother more often. So why don't you just do it? Well, I'm going to tell you my theory.

Along the way on my own journey of self-discovery, I learned the concept of *distinction*. A distinction is something that you discover that you were previously not aware of, but once you know it, you are never the same again. It's not a *learned* thing that you may forget if you don't use it all the time (for me, that would be algebra). Rather, once you discover a distinction, you will never forget it even after not using it for years. For example, do you remember learning to ride a bicycle? Whether you were trying to learn on your own or having someone help you, there was a lot of trial and error going on. But at some moment in time, you found yourself pedaling, moving forward, and not falling down! You got it! You discovered the distinction called *balance*, and once you get that distinction in your life, you will never lose it.

Another example I can use to describe the concept of distinction comes from the professional sphere. In order to function in the world of medicine, a physician needs to be able to read an x-ray. I think we've all had the experience of being at the doctor's or dentist's office when she's trying to show you what's going on with your body, and she points to an area on the x-ray and asks, *"Do you see this right here?"* I don't know what *you* do, but this is the point where I totally lie and say yes. The truth is, I think the majority of us just see some blurry, undefined shades of gray that really don't mean anything to us. To medical professionals who have learned to see things differently, however, the picture is crystal clear. They've learned a new way of seeing things, and they can never go back to *not* seeing that way. If you dropped them in a jungle in the middle of the night, blindfolded, and turned them around three times, then took off the blindfold and handed them an x-ray, they could still read it. Once they've learned how to do it, the knowledge stays with them and enables them to move forward with clarity.

So each chapter of this book is like a distinction, bringing to the surface something about yourself that is already there, but that perhaps you never saw before. And, once you see it, the knowledge will remain with you. You will now be able to look at the x-ray of your life and understand why you do what you do and why you don't do what you should. After we expose these distinctions, I'll share with you specific strategies to start designing a life worth smiling about. These are simple, easy things that you can do on a regular basis, but they are very powerful. They will alter how you feel about yourself, and they can help you create a new reality. They will help you to create a new you.

I'm going to make the assumption that no matter what you do for a living, you have to interact with other human beings. Even if you're a one-person business, you have clients and vendors. Let's assume that you want to advance in your career. What you desire could be a pay raise, more responsibility, or a different job title. One thing that's been proven in the science of smiling is that people who are happy in their life are more successful. They've mastered the art of dealing with others, and they also have the ability to handle their own stresses and frustrations. In order to succeed, you have to be skilled at the art of managing yourself, your own goals, your own actions, and your own life. If you want to master your business, you must first master yourself.

You can't possibly move others into action if you're not in action yourself. You can't possibly inspire others if you're not inspired yourself. You can't have a team of people working toward a vision or a goal if you can't do that in your own life.

Lastly, let me give you some suggestions for getting the most out of this book:

1. *Read each chapter twice before going on to the next one.* The reason for this is that when you read a chapter twice, things will sink in. There are sections of this book that will take a good amount of digesting. It's more helpful if you really let the current chapter sink deep into your subconscious before you go on to the next chapter.

2. *Ask, how does this apply to me?* As you read, frequently ask yourself how each concept fits with your life experience. See yourself and your life in the distinctions that I'm talking about.

3. *Take action now.* There are some exercises throughout this book, and I'm concerned that some of you may skip the exercises and skim through the book as if it were a novel and you were trying to find out who committed the crime. So let me save you the trouble. The secret to how to design a life worth smiling about is *not* found on the last page of the last chapter. The truth is that this book is written more as a discovery. When you do the exercises in the book, this helps prepare you for the next chapter and/or for the next exercise.

4. *Actively participate in the process.* You can write in this book, or you can use the bookmarking feature in your e-book. As you read, you may have ideas or questions that are important to you. Think of this more like a course than like something that you simply read. If you approach it that way, it will be more interactive for you, and it will help you take part in the process of discovery.

So, are you ready? Give me a big smile before you turn the page! OK . . . enjoy!

CHAPTER 1

THE SCIENCE BEHIND YOUR SMILE

A smile can brighten the darkest day.

—Author Unknown

As I began to research this book, I was amazed at how much had been written on the subject of smiling. A quick Google search will bring up hundreds of results, ranging from scientific experiments published in medical journals to lighthearted articles in health magazines. Now, some of you may have *loved* science and math when you were in high school. If you did, awesome! You're going to love this chapter. For the rest of you, bear with me through the chapter, because understanding the basics of the physical and chemical process of smiling is crucial. I'm going to give you my *very* simple version of what I learned (because I am a very simple guy), but I have to tell you that if you choose to read further about this on your own, it is really fascinating stuff.

Before I became a professional speaker, I attended many transformational seminars and training programs. When I was 20 years old, I remember one speaker saying to us in the audience: "What are feelings? Feelings are not things that you can grab onto or hold in your hand. If I were to open up your skull and look inside your brain, could I reach in there and take out a feeling? Of course not. Feelings are not things that you can control, or grab onto, or look at. They are not real things." So, that's what I was taught, and that's what I believed. But as I started to explore some of the studies that have been done on smiling and feelings,

1

I was excited to discover that, in fact, feelings *are* something that we can see (with the help of some technology). We can even control them to a certain degree. This is because what we call our feelings and emotions are basically caused by chemicals that are found in our brain, and there are certain triggers that create and release these chemicals.

As I said, I'm going to keep this as simple as possible for both of our sakes. While I spent a lot of time studying these processes, I'm not changing my title to *motivational neurosurgeon* any time soon. If, after you read this, you feel that you may be in need of brain surgery, you'll have to seek the advice of a professional.

So, let's briefly talk about the brain. When we are talking about the chemicals that regulate our emotions, there are two different parts of our brain at work—the **cortex**, which we can call our "thinking brain," and the **limbic** system, which we'll call our "emotional brain."

The **cortex** (sometimes referred to as "gray matter") is the largest part of our brain; it is responsible for memory, attention, awareness, language, and the like. It's involved in "higher thinking" and is basically what you would say makes us human. In terms of evolution, it's younger than the other parts of the brain.

The **limbic** system is more of a "group" of different parts of our brain that support a variety of functions, including emotion, behavior, motivation, and long-term memory. It's this part of the brain that's responsible for activating the "feeling" chemicals that I'm about to explain. The limbic system is older in terms of evolution. This is important to understand because a lot of our emotions and behaviors are instinctive, given to us by our ancestors. The limbic system is *all about survival.*

Chemicals That Create Feelings: DOSE

Let's take a look at the chemicals that produce our feelings. They facilitate the messages that are sent to the rest of our body when we are happy, sad, angry, depressed, excited, and so on. There are four *feel-good chemicals*: Dopamine, Oxytocin, Serotonin, and Endorphins. The acronym I created for these is DOSE. As you will see, smiling activates the release of these feel-good chemicals in the brain. You get a nice **dose** of them when a big smile flashes across your face. Let's look at what they are and how they affect our emotions.

Dopamine: The Motivation Chemical (Dream Seeker)

Dopamine can be considered the "motivator" or "reward seeker." I also like to refer to it as the "**d**ream seeker" to help me remember: **D**opamine = **D**ream. When our ancestors were living in caves and had to hunt or forage for food, dopamine was responsible for the drive that kept them looking for it again and again. For our purposes, a modern-day example would be a marathon runner seeing the finish line or a person packing his luggage for a vacation. Dopamine lets you know that either you are about to get something that you need or you are nearing a goal. It gives you that "Eureka!" feeling, and it is associated with pleasure receptors in the brain. Much reward-driven learning is based on dopamine transmission—picture a rat making its way through a maze because it knows that a piece of cheese is waiting at the end. Many highly addictive drugs, including stimulants such as cocaine and methamphetamine, act directly on the brain's dopamine receptors. The personality traits that some people would call "outgoing" or "attention seeking" may have something to do with a higher sensitivity of the dopamine system.

Dopamine Dream Seeker

How does smiling fit into this? Studies have shown that when we smile, we get a shot of dopamine. It's been said that the feeling one gets from smiling is equivalent to the feeling of winning a lottery ticket of $25,000.[1] Sounds great, right?

I'm going to try this the next time I go to the bank to pay my mortgage. With a couple of flashes of my pearly whites, I figure I'll have my home paid off by next week! LOL.

Oxytocin: The Love Chemical (Others)

Oxytocin is referred to as the "love hormone." It activates your ability to trust, act more generously, and become more social with others. It is associated with bonding. It can be released by a physical action like holding hands, but it is also released when there is a perceived type of bonding, such as your comments being "liked" on a social media network. (You folks who are my Facebook friends had no idea that you were my oxytocin dealers, did you?) Even being part of a crowd at a concert or sports arena promotes this "belonging" chemical. To help you remember what **O**xytocin is, think of the *o* as meaning "**O**thers."

Oxytocin Relationships

Oxytocin also plays a role in childbirth, as large amounts are released during labor, during a mother's first contact with her newborn, and during breast feeding.[2] I can't think of a more powerful example of bonding than that.

When you smile at someone and get a smile back—whether it is from a loved one or a stranger—you will get a dose of oxytocin as your urge to belong and connect with others is fulfilled. This is true in the office as well as in your personal life. For instance, if you smile while you're negotiating with another businessperson, you'll achieve better results because you're building trust and triggering the release of a healthy dose of oxytocin for you both.

Serotonin: The Survival Chemical (Status)

When you think about our limbic system and how it is concerned with our survival, you could say that serotonin is the chemical force that drives us to seek elevated status (**S**erotonin = **S**tatus). Dominant males and females have a better chance of mating, therefore enabling their DNA to survive. We're not consciously thinking about our gene pool when we seek respect from our peers, but we do get a big dose of serotonin when we're praised or when we're in the limelight. Picture the "alpha" dog in a pack. He has a calm, self-assured sense of his place in the big scheme of things, and he likes it! Serotonin is associated with our ability to deal with group dynamics and competition.

Serotonin Survival

Serotonin also plays a role as a transmitter, helping to smoothly relay messages from one part of the brain to another. When there is a lack or imbalance of serotonin, these relays can't function properly, sometimes resulting in depression. Many of the well-known antidepressant medications (such as Prozac and Zoloft) focus on correcting this relay "glitch" with serotonin.

The simple act of flashing a smile (activating those facial muscles) will trigger a release of serotonin. You don't need a prescription, and there are no negative side effects. Imagine the difference it would make in our society if people understood this very simple fact! Instead of relying on a prescription to fix all of our troubles, and rather than turning to drugs or alcohol, we should all practice smiling more often.

Endorphins: The Antistress Chemicals (Energy)

Endorphins are the chemicals that are responsible for what we call a "runner's high." When released, they act on the same receptors in the brain as opiate drugs do and produce a euphoric feeling just as morphine does. They are our body's natural way to mask pain. So whenever we need a little extra boost of energy (Endorphins = Energy) to deal with physical or emotional stress, or to overcome an obstacle, our body asks for more endorphins.

Endorphin Energy

For example, endorphins are released during sex and when eating certain foods, such as chili peppers and chocolate. When it comes to the peppers, the spicier, the better. More pain means more chemical. Now, chocolate doesn't cause any pain whatsoever, but research has shown that it also triggers endorphins, probably because of the surge of energy that we get from eating sugar. This may also explain the comforting feelings that many people associate with it, and the craving for chocolate in times of stress. (By the way, according to the British Dental Health Foundation, smiling is equivalent to eating 2,000 bars of chocolate[3] . . . without the calories [and the cavities]! I know this made some readers *very* happy.)

To Summarize . . . DOSE

What's important for you to recognize is that your brain needs a fix of these chemicals—and in a serious way! And because our brains are automatic, chemically controlled goal-seeking devices, they'll find a way to get a DOSE, whether it's a productive way (winning a game, finishing a major project, going out on a date, or landing a sale) or a destructive way (drugs, bad relationships, addictions, acting out to get attention, or constant complaining). Both good and bad activities can release a DOSE; wouldn't it be far better to simply smile?

Our brains have become trained through our life experiences, like a well-worn path through a forest. We continue to follow the same trail—even if it's not particularly good for us—because it's literally the path of least resistance and leads us back to our comfort zone and our chemical DOSE "reward."

Now that you have an understanding of the four feel-good chemicals that create our feelings, let's take a closer look at what smiling is and how it plays an important role in our happiness.

The Duchenne Smile

I wonder how many of you just said, "Oh, no! Here comes a French lesson." Well, we have to understand the concept of the *Duchenne smile*, since it is so prevalent in the science of smiling.

During his research on facial expressions in the mid-nineteenth century, French physician Guillaume Duchenne (pronounced dew-SHEN) identified two distinct types of smiles: the *Duchenne smile* and the *forced smile*.[4] The smile that is named after Duchenne involves contraction of both the major muscles that raise the corners of the mouth and the muscles that raise the cheeks and form crow's feet around the eyes; this is the smile that you don't think about. This type of smile is totally unconscious and automatic—the one that lights up your face just before you burst out laughing. It appears when you see your first child born or when someone who you've admired from afar asks you out on a date. It's the one you'll see on children's faces when they're playing a game and laughing with their friends.

The most important components of the Duchenne smile are the muscles around the eyes. I love how the well-known model and celebrity Tyra Banks calls it "smize," as in when you "smile" with your "eyes." I sometimes refer to this as an "authentic smile."

The other type of smile is a forced smile. It's not automatic; it's contrived. It's that awkward kind of smile that just doesn't make its way to the eyes. (Think of high school yearbook pictures.) We all do it at one time or another. Because it's a forced smile, it uses fewer muscles than the Duchenne smile, but hey, some muscles are better than none.

Now, while the next few sections will show you that *any* type of smile can have a positive effect on your mood and well-being, my goal in this book is to show you how to have more moments in your life that create authentic smiles.

Can Simply Smiling Make You Happy?

In our research on smiling, we learned something very interesting. We often think that smiling is a result of feeling good, but studies show that our smiles *themselves* can make us feel good! The so-called formula for success, then, is scientifically backward. We are programmed to think that only "when I get the new car, house, promotion, money, or whatever," will I have less stress and smile more. Actually, it's the other way around. As the Zen Buddhist monk Thich Nhat Hanh says, "*Sometimes your joy is the source of your smile, but sometimes your smile can be the source of your joy.*" Here are a few studies that validate this.

The Muscles Behind the Smile

Now that we know that a smile can affect the chemistry in our brain, which in turn can help us have less stress and feel happier in our lives, let's take a look at the mechanics of our facial expressions, and why simply putting these muscles to work will give us a DOSE of those awesome feel-good chemicals. I'm sure you've heard the expression, "It takes more muscles to frown than it does to smile." *Not true.* We have more than 40 muscles in our face[5] that can create literally thousands of different facial expressions (unless you're Joan Rivers, in which case you have only four facial expressions—*love ya, Joan!*). If we analyze a forced smile, it raises only the corners of the lips. There are a total of ten muscles that accomplish this; four muscles raise the upper lip, while six more raise the corners of the mouth. To take this a step further, we know that an authentic smile (the Duchenne smile) also involves the muscles around the eyes, which is a total of approximately 12 muscles.

Now let's take a look at a frown. When we frown or when we're sad, what do we do with our face? Well, we actually relax it, mainly using the two muscles in our lower lip and the four muscles around the corners of our mouth to lower them. That's a total of six. So, it takes 6 muscles to frown; 10 muscles are needed for a forced smile; and an authentic smile uses 12 or more. Have you ever gone to a comedy club and spent so much time smiling and laughing the whole night that you end up saying, "Oh my gosh; my face is still hurting." That's because you gave your muscles a workout!

This is precisely why we need to *keep* smiling as often as we can. What do you do when you want to be stronger so that you can lift heavier things? What do you do when you're training yourself to run longer distances, or to run faster? You go to the gym and you work out those specific muscles. You're actually altering and strengthening those particular muscles, and this eventually changes the way you look. Well, we have to do the same thing with the muscles in our face. *When you smile more often, you're actually altering the way your face looks in a positive, attractive way . . . and it's free!*

Facial Expression Studies

Most of us think that our facial expressions represent our mood. In other words, we have the feeling *first*, and then we tell our face to express that feeling. But *what if* our face can tell our brain how it should feel? Eric Finzi, a dermatologic surgeon and coauthor of a study on frowning, points out, "You can influence mental health by what you do with your face, whether you smile more or frown less."[6] So, *what if* our face can tell our brain how it should feel? That's the question that the next few studies have tried to answer.

Biting a Pencil

In 1988, researcher Fritz Strack and his team wanted to see whether smiling could in fact change your mood.[7] As part of their study, they told the participants that they were studying adaptations for people who had lost the use of their hands, and would need to use their mouths to hold pencils for writing. The story was necessary for the study, so that the subjects would not know that they were being made to "smile."

The researchers had the participants hold a pencil in their mouth, either in their teeth (which activates the muscles used for smiling) or just in their lips (which does not activate those muscles), and then had them read cartoons and rate them based on how funny they were. Those who were (unknowingly) "smiling" rated the cartoons as funnier than people who weren't smiling.

So, what was happening here? How does biting a pencil change your perception? The idea is simple: your brain is constantly monitoring what's happening in your body. When it analyzes things like your facial expression, posture, and muscle tension, it can "judge" how you're feeling. By putting your face in a happier position (using the same muscles that a smile uses), you can boost your mood. Holding a pencil between your teeth mimics a genuine smile because it activates the same muscles of the mouth, cheeks, and eyes. It's almost as if your brain sees your face smiling and says, "Hey, I don't know what's going on down there, but we're smiling about something, so we must be happy! Quick: send out some endorphins and serotonin on the double!"

Facial Feedback Theory

The *facial feedback theory* is basically the idea that *your facial expressions can affect, or even cause, your mood.* There have been many different studies done on this subject. The theory goes back to Charles Darwin, who first suggested in the nineteenth century[8] that your "emotional experience must be accompanied by an appropriate muscular activity." He proposed that your facial expressions aren't just displaying your feelings, but may actually *determine* your mental state. During the 1970s and 1980s, there were many studies published that supported this theory of facial feedback.

According to the *New York Times*, "In 1984, Dr. Paul Ekman and other psychologists at the University of California Medical School at San Francisco published an article in the journal *Science* showing that when people mimic different emotional expressions, their bodies produce distinctive physiological patterns, such as changes in heart and breath rate, for each emotion."[9] According to Dr. Ekman, a deep, authentic smile (a Duchenne smile) "generates the physiology of positive emotion and the changes in the brain' associated with spontaneous enjoyment."[10]

In the study, one group of subjects was shown pictures of various facial expressions, another group made those facial expressions, and a final group made those expressions while looking in the mirror.

Subjects were asked questions that pinpointed their emotional state after each test. The two groups that actually made the facial expressions scored overwhelmingly happier after the test, whereas the one group that only looked at pictures of these facial expressions had no change at all. Those in the group that smiled in the mirror saw an even more pronounced change in mood than those in the group that smiled without the mirror. The evidence all points toward smiling as a *cause* (rather than a result) of happy feelings.

Another study showing how your face can tell your brain that you're feeling good was conducted by Dr. Robert Zajonc, a psychologist at the University of Michigan.[11] He had the subjects repeat vowel sounds that forced their faces into various expressions. To mimic the characteristics of a smile, they made the long *e* sound, stretching the corners of the mouth outward. Other vowel sounds were also tested, including the long *u*, which forces the mouth into a pouty expression. The subjects reported feeling good after making the long *e* sound and feeling bad after the long *u*. Just saying the letter *eeee* makes your brain think you're smiling! So, go ahead and pretend I'm about to take your picture right now. What would you say? Try it, nice and loud: 1 . . . 2 . . . 3 . . . *cheeeese*! You just got yourself a dose of happiness.

The Epitome of Empathy

This study, conducted by Dr. Zajonc, shows that mimicking another person's face over time can actually change the way you look.[12] The study asked a group of people to view two dozen photos of newlyweds and two dozen photos of couples who had been married for 25 years or longer. These were individual pictures, not pictures of the two people together. He then asked the group to try to match up the couples. The researchers found that the newlyweds might or might not have shown any similarity to each other, but that there was a definite resemblance between the couples who had been married 25 years or more. Although the resemblances were not dramatic (merely subtle shifts in facial wrinkles and other facial contours), they were apparent enough that the subjects were able to match up the older couples more accurately.

Dr. Zajonc theorizes that when a spouse empathizes with her partner and mimics her partner's facial expression, it can actually change the appearance of the person's own face, over time. How's that for empathy?! I guess the longer you stay married, and the more you are in sync with your partner and his feelings; the more the two of you really *do* start to look like each other.

How Botox Affects Smiling, Feelings, and Communication

There have been findings about Botox and smiling that are pretty intriguing. By the way, in case you live in a cave or don't get the Bravo cable network to watch *The Real Housewives*, let's make sure we all understand what Botox really does. First of all, Botox is just the most popular brand name. It's actually a bacterial product (botulinum toxin) that temporarily paralyzes the muscle into which it is injected. Did you read what I just wrote? *It paralyzes the muscles* in the face. Can you guess where we are going with this?

One study[13] showed how Botox can inhibit the ability to mimic the facial expressions of others, therefore affecting how we communicate. Being able to *mirror* others' feelings helps us to understand what someone is experiencing. So, with the introduction of Botox, the ability to display this nonverbal communication is reduced, and this can be misinterpreted as a lack of empathy, which can stand in the way of our connecting with others.

Professor Rod Sinclair, director of dermatology at Epworth Hospital and the University of Melbourne, said that other people read our facial expressions to pick up our mood, so that, if anything, having Botox could influence the way people react to us.[14]

"If you had too much Botox, then you wouldn't communicate your mood very well, and that would probably have an impact on how other people react to you," he said.

So you can see that paralyzing the muscles in your face that are involved in smiling can affect not only how you feel, but also how people relate to you. If they think that you're not being empathetic, you may be sending them the wrong message, which will most certainly affect your communication with them.

When Dr. Michael Lewis from Cardiff University asked patients who had had Botox injections in the muscles around their eyes to diminish crow's feet (the same muscles used in a Duchenne smile), to fill out a questionnaire, he found that these patients were more likely to have feelings of depression, compared to those who had treatment only for their forehead lines. Dr. Lewis suggested that using Botox on crow's feet decreased the "strength of a smile," so people felt less happy. He also noted that the opposite can be true, such as when he studied patients who had only the frown lines on their forehead removed. "If you can't frown any more, you end up feeling happier," Dr. Lewis said. "It's called facial feedback. The expressions we make on our face are connected to the emotions we feel."[15]

In a separate study on frowning, Dr. Eric Finzi injected Botox[16] into the frown muscles of half of a group of 74 people diagnosed with depression, preventing these patients from frowning. The other half received placebo injections. After six weeks, 27 percent of the Botox patients went into remission for their depression. That compares with a 7 percent remission rate for the patients in the control group.

A Cool Brain Is a Happy Brain

Dr. Robert Zajonc conducted a study[17] about why your facial muscles may trigger a feeling of happiness. He tested this theory by looking at what is actually happening to the blood flow in your face when these muscles are activated. Smiling causes certain facial muscles to stretch and tighten, with the result that veins are constricted. These veins in your face lead to your carotid artery, which carries the majority of the blood that is delivered to your brain. A lower volume of blood means a drop in temperature.

There are already numerous studies suggesting that having a warmer brain is associated with negative emotions and unpleasant feelings, while having a cooler brain is linked to positive emotions and pleasant feelings. (So people who get angry a lot and turn red in the face really are "hotheads" after all!)

"I'm not saying that all moods are due to changes in the muscles of the face, only that facial action leads to changes in mood," said Dr. Zajonc.

His research even goes further to suggest that the size of your smile is important, because a very broad smile will constrict the muscles more than an average smile, thus dropping the volume of blood, lowering the temperature, and increasing your brain's "happiness." Isn't that cool?

(Just a Few) Specific Benefits of Smiling

There are a number of specific benefits of smiling, several of which are discussed here.

Smiling Is Contagious

Imagine this scenario: you're at a cocktail party, milling around and chatting here and there—the same as everyone else. The atmosphere is, well, pleasant enough. Now picture a new person entering the room— let's say a man, although it really doesn't matter—who has this huge, warm, genuine smile on his face as he starts to walk around and talk to people. Watch what happens as he begins to engage with others— how the energy changes. As the old saying goes, it's as if this person is "lighting up the room." You can see the change happening as other people begin to mirror this person's expression. It's totally unconscious; I mean, people literally cannot help but smile back. A single person can start this type of chain reaction with a single smile.

You know the song "When You're Smiling" ("When you're smilin' keep on smilin' The whole world smiles with you") made famous by Louis Armstrong in 1929? Well, it seems that there is some scientific basis to those lyrics. Many studies have shown that something as simple as seeing a friend smile can activate the muscles in your face to make that same expression, without your even being aware that you are doing it.

In one Swedish study,[18] subjects were shown pictures of people exhibiting several emotions: *joy, anger, fear,* and *surprise.* When a photo of a person who was smiling was presented, the researchers asked the subjects to frown, but they noticed that the subjects' *initial reaction* upon seeing the photo was to smile. They had to make a conscious effort to "turn that smile upside down." So, when you smile at others, and they don't return the favor, it's likely they're making a conscious decision not to.

As we discussed a few pages back, "mirroring" is a natural technique that humans use when communicating with each other. It has been shown that "mimicking other people's behavior is an important mechanism of bonding in group situations," according to Evan Carr from the Department of Psychology at the University of California, San Diego.[19] It's as if each time you smile at a person, that person's brain coaxes him to return the favor. You are creating a symbiotic relationship that allows both of you to release some feel-good chemicals in your brain and activate those "reward center" receptors.

The tricky part of this mirroring phenomenon is that when someone is frowning, it can be just as contagious. You know the saying, "misery loves company"? Volunteers in studies have reported actually experiencing the moods that they were asked to portray on their faces.

So, if our facial expressions can be a factor in determining our mood, and if frowning is also contagious, how do we avoid "catching" these negative vibes? Don't worry; knowing how to identify negativity and deflect it is dealt with in a later chapter. For now, just know that if you choose to smile, you are almost guaranteed that the world will smile back!

Smiling Reduces Stress

I don't think I need to tell you about the negative effects that stress can have on you, both mentally and physically. Literally hundreds, if not thousands, of studies and books have been written on the subject. One of the ways to measure stress is by monitoring your blood pressure and/or heart rate. There was a study done at the University of Kansas[20] to measure the effects of smiling on the body's ability to recover from stress. It's a long study, but I will try to summarize it for you in a nutshell.

Scientists Tara Kraft and Sarah Pressman wanted to measure the potential benefits of smiling by looking at how different types of smiling, and the awareness of smiling, affect individuals' ability to recover from episodes of stress.

They took 169 college students (hooked up to a monitor to measure their heart rate) and told them that they were participating in an experiment on multitasking. Their first task was to trace a star-shaped design (easy enough, right?) with their nondominant hand (hmmm), and they had to do it while seeing only their hand's reverse image in a mirror (what??). To add even more pressure, the researchers told the students that accuracy was important, and they gave them false statistics about the "average" performance.

The students were given two minutes to do this, and then had five minutes of downtime. For the next part of the experiment, they were asked to submerge one of their hands in ice water for one minute, and then they had another five-minute recovery period. Remember, their heart rate was being monitored the whole time. Now, here's the kicker.

During these tasks, these students *also* had been put into five groups based on facial expression. Before the tests, the students in each group were told that they had to shape their face in a particular way while they were performing the task. They were shown photos of how their faces should look and were given chopsticks to hold in their mouths.

These were the groups: (1) neutral expression, (2) standard smiling, (3) standard smiling without being told that they were smiling (that is, being instructed to position their facial muscles in a particular way, but without calling it a smile), (4) Duchenne smiling, and (5) Duchenne smiling without being told that they were smiling.

After measuring the elevated heart rates and recovery time, here's what they found. Regardless of whether or not they were *aware* that they were smiling, the smiling participants recovered from stress more quickly than those with neutral expressions, and those displaying Duchenne smiles recovered a bit more quickly than those displaying a standard smile.

"We wanted to examine whether smiling could have real health-relevant benefits," said Kraft.

We can think of smiling as a sort of anti-inflammatory drug. Here's what I mean. If you sprain your ankle or wrist, you may get a prescription to reduce the swelling so that you can heal more quickly. Well, *smiling reduces the swelling of negative feelings* and also helps you to recover more quickly.

I wanted to put this theory to the test myself, so I ordered a home blood pressure testing device (I love Amazon). I took my blood pressure first without any facial expressions; I was very stoic. Then I took the test again, but this time I smiled while the device took my readings. I did this quite a number of times, at different times of the day and in different locations. Of course, I needed other test subjects, so I chased my family around, trying to run the test on them. I actually annoyed the members of my family so much that they made me send the machine back (totally true story). Anyway, let's talk about the results of my own "highly scientific" study. As I said, I did this several times, and my blood pressure readings came back lower when I was smiling than when I wasn't in 80 percent of the tests. I think that's pretty amazing!

Smiling Lets You Look Younger—Without Surgery

Forget all these expensive anti-aging creams; a simple smile can have you looking several years younger instantly.

Researchers from the Max Planck Institute in Berlin[21] found that smiling people were "more attractive, and had a more youthful appearance than their solemn counterparts."

This study had 150 men and women look at more than 1,000 photos of faces and guess the age of the person in each photo. The responses were most accurate when the facial expression was neutral. If the face was smiling, the participants guessed that the person in the photo was younger than his or her actual age.

"Facial expression has a substantial impact on accuracy," says Manuel Voelkle from the study. "Those displaying happy expressions were most likely underestimated."

After learning how our brain detects and interprets facial expression, I had a thought about this theory. If I asked you the question, "Who has more stress in their life—children or adults?" I think it's safe to say that almost all of you would say "adults." So, besides the obvious visual benefit that a smiling face keeps us from *looking* tired and worn down, we subconsciously associate a "worry-free" face with youth.

Smiling Lets You Be More Attractive

OK, for some of you this is a very important part of the book. It's not that I'm suggesting that you are personally in need of improvement, but you may know people in your life who are really not all that attractive, and who need every bit of help they can get. So, all I'm saying is that you should feel free to pass along this information.

As superficial as this may sound, and as much as we may not want it to be true, it is a known phenomenon that people who are perceived as physically attractive are treated differently. But here's some great news! No matter what the structure of your face, you look more attractive to others when you smile. Studies have shown that "smilers" are viewed as more attractive, reliable, relaxed, and sincere.

A study published in *Neuropsychologia*, an international journal of behavioral and cognitive neuroscience,[22] reported that seeing an attractive, smiling face activates your orbitofrontal cortex (boy, that's a mouthful). This is the region in your brain that processes sensory rewards. It suggests that when you view a person who is smiling, you actually feel rewarded. Did you read that? *When you are smiling, people feel like you're rewarding them!* Wow.

It also explains findings by researchers at the Face Research Laboratory at the University of Aberdeen, Scotland.[23] Subjects were asked to rate smiling and attractiveness, and they found that both men and women were more attracted to images of people who made eye contact and smiled than to those who did not. If you don't believe me, do your own research. The next time you are out and about, notice how many looks you get if you walk around with a big grin on your face. (Not too big—you don't want people to stare at you, just to notice your positive way of being.)

Did you ever wonder why we're always asked to smile in photos? It's because people usually look their best—and their happiest—when they are smiling. According to the American Academy of Cosmetic Dentistry,[24] 96 percent of American adults believe that an attractive smile makes a person more appealing to members of the opposite sex.

A research study done by Orbit Complete[25] discovered that a whopping 69 percent of people find a makeup-free, smiling face more attractive than a makeup-wearing, nonsmiling one.

One study examined how men approached women in a bar.[26] When a woman only established eye contact with a man, she was approached 20 percent of the time. When the same woman added a smile, though, she was approached 60 percent of the time. When I read that I thought to myself, "Duh!" So, ladies, smiling at a man is magical . . . and it's certainly a way to attract attention, if that's what you're aiming to do. It shows that you're open, receptive, and willing to engage in further communication.

I'll share another study with you, though, so that you don't think I'm totally biased. This one showed that when men smile at women, the effect is not quite as magical. There's some evidence to show that smiling less makes a man look more masculine, and that men may appear more attractive to women when they are displaying pride, or even shame, than when they look happy.[27] So men, maybe don't walk up to a woman in a bar smiling from ear to ear and ready to buy her a drink. You may get maced.

One last thought on this. Remember how I said earlier that it takes more muscles to smile than to frown, and that the more you work those muscles, the easier it is to smile, just like going to the gym? Well, the stronger you keep those facial muscles, the tighter your face is, which helps prevent sagging, droopy skin. This is like a noninvasive surgical facelift without the expense.

You gotta love this smile thing!

Smiling Helps You Make More Money

If you're in the business of selling, or if your company has face-to-face interactions with customers, you'll want to pay attention to the next studies.

As you know, in any sales situation, it's important that the customer is able to trust the person who is doing the selling. One signal that suggests that someone is trustworthy is a smile. Genuine smiles send a message that others can rely on and that leads them to cooperate with us.[28]

There is a financial return for that smile, too. Researchers at Bangor University[29] have placed an economic value on a smile, scientifically demonstrating the effect that a genuine smile can have on our decision making. The study's psychologists call this "social information" and say that it has more of an effect than you may imagine.

Danielle Shore, a PhD candidate at the Bangor University School of Psychology and lead author of the research, provided an interesting analogy centered on buying a new car. The analyst contends that your impression of the salesperson is an even larger factor in your purchase decision than the features of the automobile itself, such as running cost or reliability. In fact, they found that when buyers perceive a genuine smile from a salesperson, they are inclined to buy a more expensive vehicle or to add more options than they originally planned.

The advertising world realizes just how much smiling can affect consumers' spending habits. One marketing research study[30] showed participants a few picture ads, then asked for their opinions. These ads showed a model either with or without an authentic (Duchenne) smile.

When the model displayed a Duchenne smile, the participants were more willing to buy the product and to pay higher prices for it. Moreover, these results were consistent for both expensive (for example, a laptop) and inexpensive (for example, a sandwich) products. The researchers concluded that seeing an ad in which the model had a Duchenne smile primed people with a positive emotional response, which leaked over to the product.

This type of subtle "priming" happens all the time, and even small changes in the way a salesperson, spokesperson, or model smiles may have an impact on how you spend your money.

If you're about to go on a job interview, you may think that all that matters about your appearance is the clothes you are wearing. Wrong! You can't just put on a nice outfit; you have to put on a nice smile as well. In a study published in the December 2009 issue of *Personality and Social Psychology Bulletin*,[31] people looked at full-body photographs of 123 people they had never met. The people in the photos had one of two expressions: neutral or a smile. And guess what? When observers saw a photo of a smiling person, they were more likely to think that the person in the photo was likable, confident, conscientious, and stable. Sound like traits that most companies want in an employee, right? So the next time you're dressing to impress, make sure to take that beautiful, natural smile with you!

Smiling Improves Customer Service

Certain industries and companies realize just how crucial the simple act of smiling can be for customer service and satisfaction. There are service jobs (such as flight attendants, for example, or those in the hospitality business) for which employees are trained in the importance of smiling. Have you ever been on a plane where there was one passenger who was being incredibly needy or just out-and-out rude to the flight attendant? (Hopefully, this was not you!) I'd be willing to bet you that the flight attendant kept smiling through the whole encounter.

In fact, staying with this industry, there's even an airline called THAI Smile (www.thaismileair.com). On its website, it says, "Travel with THAI Smile is designed to be vibrant, fun, speedy, trendy and friendly the moment you step onboard." It goes on to explain each and every one of those terms, and makes sure to say that every aspect of the airline, from booking to check-in to food and beverage to baggage, is "all provided with a genuine smile." How great is that?

And what about the people who work at any Disney park (the cast members)? They're the total opposite of the royal guards outside of Buckingham Palace. You can't stop these people from smiling! As part of their job duties, they are expected to always keep a big grin on their faces when they are interacting with the public.

In Japanese culture, where the client is king, customer service can make or break your business. One company, Omron, has taken this concept to a whole new level, thanks to face recognition technology. It was the first to develop a high-tech "Smile Scan"[32] that uses sensors to capture an image of a person's face and gauge the degree of the person's smile from zero to 100 percent.

Keikyu, a private rail operator in Tokyo, started to use this "smile check" for the first time soon after the Smile Scan was unveiled in 2009.[33] Before starting work, the staff members have to smile into a camera; in the best case, they collect 100 points. The pictures are saved in the system, and each time an employee smiles at the camera, it is compared with that employee's best-ever smile.

"We usually have a lot to do in the morning," said one employee. "When this was originally introduced, I thought, 'Great, another thing on my plate.' I was very skeptical. But since I have started doing it, I have noticed that it does actually improve my mood. So I think it is a good thing now."

Keikyu is not the only company in Japan that trains its staff in friendliness. Omron has sold its "smile-o-meters" to insurance companies, banks, hospitals, and other firms.

Smiling Helps You Live Longer

Ernest L. Abel and Michael L. Kruger at Wayne State University have found that the larger your smile, the longer you may live. Yes, that's right; "smile intensity" seems to have a statistically significant effect on a person's longevity.

In their research,[34] the professors conducted an amusing case study that used a sampling of 230 photographs of baseball players culled from the now-defunct *Sporting News Baseball Register*. The professional ball-players were chosen as a representative sample because detailed life statistics (such as birth, death, education, marital status, and the like) were available for each, leading to a more conclusive study.

The players' headshots, taken in the lead-up to the 1952 season, were analyzed by the researchers and their assistants and given flat determinations of either "no smile," "partial smile," or "authentic large (Duchenne) smile." After some web research, the analysts compiled the life data for the baseball players and controlled for body mass index, career length, marital status, college attendance, and other longevity factors.

The results? Even a partial smile added years to a player's lifespan. On average, the players with no smile lived for 72.9 years, the players with partial smiles lived an average of 74.9 years, and the players with the big full smile—wait for it—lived an average of 79.9 years. That's a seven-year difference! And the main evidence to go on was whether photos typically showed players smiling, and to what degree. Amazing!

Based on this, I've come up with a legal way to kill someone you don't like. (I'm kidding here, of course.) But check this out: when you have a confrontation with people you don't like, and they're yelling at you, do *not* yell back—just smile. Here's what happens: they're angry already, and you're just there smiling, and because you're smiling, you're living longer. Now, at the same time, they are getting angrier *because* you are smiling at them, which makes their life shorter. This, of course, makes you smile even more, which means that you add even more years to your life! So I say, "Kill them with kindness" (or smiling, in this case).

Smiling Helps You Have a Better Marriage

Lee Anne Harker and Dacher Keltner[35] conducted a long-term study examining women's yearbook pictures at an elite institution in relation to a variety of life outcomes, including health, personality, and marriage. They calculated the intensity of female students' smiles in their senior yearbook photo. How did they know that the smiles weren't being faked? They used computer technology to measure 44 aspects of facial activity. If a smile were not genuine, certain muscles were not active.

Throughout their adult lives, the subjects completed assessments for the study. The researchers discovered that the more intense the subject's positive expression in her senior yearbook picture, the more likely it was that she would be married by age 27 and that she would have a more satisfying marriage in adulthood. Furthermore, she was likely to be more organized, content, nurturing, compassionate, and sociable than those women with less intense smiles. "This means that we can take photos at a wedding, and from them we may be able to tell how the marriage will go," said Dr. Keltner.

Smiling Is Universal

Anthropologists, biologists, and psychologists agree that smiles are globally recognized. Around the world, a true, authentic, squinty-eyed smile is recognized as a sign of happiness.

In a famous study,[36] psychologists showed that people all over the world use the same facial expressions to convey basic emotions. In studying an isolated tribe from the highlands of New Guinea, the researchers told stories to the tribe members (using a translator) describing different emotions, such as happiness, sadness, fear, and disgust. When they showed the tribe members a series of pictures of facial expressions, they were able to match the picture to the story.

Other research has demonstrated that emotional facial expressions are innate. Those born blind, for instance, smile just like sighted individuals, despite the fact that they've never seen a happy face to mimic.[37]

So well understood is the act of smiling that it has been said that **humans can detect a smile from more than 300 feet away.** This is more than twice the distance at which we can distinguish other facial expressions. The supposition is that this ability evolved so that we could determine friend from foe quickly and take appropriate action. Likewise, there are several studies that report that a smile somehow makes us feel that a complete stranger looks familiar.[38] It's just that comforting!

So, now that you understand a bit about the science of smiling and see just how deeply ingrained this is within our DNA, I want to share with you specific tips and techniques that will enable you to proactively design a life that's worth smiling about.

CHAPTER 2

WHAT'S THAT VOICE IN MY HEAD, AND HOW CAN I MAKE IT STOP?

The thought manifests as the word; the word manifests as the deed; the deed develops into habit; habit hardens into character. So watch the thought and its ways with care.

—Buddha

So, now that you've learned about all those studies in the previous chapter, I'm going to assume that you're on the smiling bandwagon with me, and that you agree that there are many ways in which smiling can benefit both you and the people around you. Of course, you may be saying to yourself, "Great, but what am I supposed to do? Just walk around like a guinea pig biting on pencils and eating chocolate?" Well, based on the science, doing this *would* certainly give you a happiness boost, but only temporarily. Fortunately, I have a much better plan in mind.

I'd like to show you how to design a life for yourself that gives you many more reasons to smile—naturally—every day. But before we can move down that road, we have to get a few things out of the way. Let me explain.

Here's my basic observation about all human beings:

There are things we should do that if we did them, would make our lives better, and there are things we shouldn't do that if we didn't do them, would make our lives better.

If you break it down to its very essence, the formula for achieving a desired outcome in anything is to take action.

| Actions | Produce | Results |

It's that simple. If you perform a particular action, you will produce a particular result. And *yes*, if you take *no* action, that still counts as an action. *Not* doing something (choosing *inaction*) will still produce a particular result. So, here's my question: If it's that simple, then *why oh why* do we continue to do the things we shouldn't and *not* do the things we should?

What stops us from taking the actions that we know would benefit us?

To help illustrate this idea, let's look at the biting a pencil study we spoke about earlier. If you now know that biting a pencil will release the feel-good chemicals in your brain and help you to feel less stressed, why wouldn't you do it when you need to? What would hold you back from doing something that would make you feel better? Could it be that:

* You think you'll look stupid.
* You think people will laugh at you.
* You don't think the study makes any sense.

Let's take another example. Say you want to make more money. There are several obvious actions you could take that might help you to achieve this. For instance, you could ask for a raise. You could update your résumé and submit it to recruiters. You could go back to school to earn a degree that qualifies you for higher earnings. These are all valid approaches, and they would be likely to produce the desired result. So, what would stop you from taking one or more of these steps?

* You think your boss will say no.
* You don't actually think you're worth it.
* You think the job market and the economy are against you.
* You think you're too old to go back to school.

Do you see the common thread here? The thing that gets in the way of your taking action is your *thoughts*. Your thoughts are very powerful. They are what stand between you and the things you want most, the things that will make your life worth smiling about.

The first important thing to realize about your thoughts is that they *never* stop talking to you! There is literally a nonstop conversation going on inside your head. Check it out for yourself. Stop reading for a few seconds and pay attention to that little voice in your head. What's it saying to you right now? I bet the first thing it said was, "OK, what am I supposed to hear? What little voice?" Yup, that's it. There are many different names for it: inner voice, internal speech, stream of consciousness. These thoughts influence both our feelings and the actions that we take. We allow them to tell us what we can and cannot do, what's possible and what isn't, and what actions we should take or not take. Our thoughts literally control all aspects of our life.

Where It All Began

From the second we're born, our brains are compiling, recording, and analyzing a huge amount of input. These are the experiences that we collectively call our "lives." We're totally unaware of this process; it's completely automatic.

When we spoke about the science of smiling, we established that our limbic system automatically releases chemicals in response to external clues. We don't consciously have to say, "Hey, Brain, I'm eating a hot fudge sundae; get those endorphins pumping"—it just happens. While this is occurring, our "thinking brain" is also taking notes on each particular event, and we're not controlling this, either. When we have an experience, our brain records it, along with the chemicals (and feelings) associated with it. You don't have to consciously do anything at all—just keep going about your business and your brain will take care of everything! Efficient system, right? Not really.

The problem with this process is that as we grow up, our past experiences naturally program us to think about ourselves and the world around us in a particular way. This conditioning becomes our ordinary way of thinking and perpetuates itself in our daily lives. Let me give you an example of how this might affect you today.

Maybe one morning you're at an office meeting, and you bring up a new idea that you have, but your boss or a colleague quickly dismisses it. In that moment, how do you feel? Embarrassed, probably, or even a little angry. But those emotions pass, and you go on with your day. It really wasn't all that traumatic for you, but make no mistake: your brain made its little note, which looks something like this:

Putting Yourself Out There = Vulnerable = Uncomfortable = Bad

The interesting thing to recognize here is that when your idea was rejected at the meeting, your brain actually associated it with "that time in the second grade when I raised my hand and everybody laughed because I had the wrong answer." This connection happened within milliseconds. That "feeling" you had while you were sitting in that conference room, as an adult, surged at lightning speed down the same exact neural pathway that was created when you were seven years old.

As a matter of fact, let's take this even further and say that this particular pathway is a well-traveled one—it's basically the "rejection expressway." This is the same road your brain took when you tried out for your high school play and your best friend got the lead instead of you, and again when your college sweetheart decided that maybe you two should "just be friends." You see, your brain does not differentiate between your *idea* being rejected at the meeting and you *yourself* feeling rejected. Every time you experience this feeling that is identified with rejection, it strengthens the neural pathway that is involved. This pathway, once it's created, will stay there. You cannot undo it. It's set in mental concrete. But there's good news: you can create an alternative, more beneficial pathway that works on your behalf.

It is important for you to understand this concept, because as we go through the book, I'm going to give you some suggestions that will help you to create new pathways. Happiness, successes, and accomplishments—these are the beneficial pathways that we want to carve out and strengthen. We do this by learning and repeating positive actions that pay us with a DOSE of our feel-good chemicals.

Now, sometimes your brain will make connections that make no sense at all. This is what some people would politely call "letting your thoughts wander." Picture yourself in your car going to work, but you're sitting in traffic because there's construction taking place. Let's listen in on the conversation in your head.

> "Ugh. Great. Why can't they do this construction at night when people don't have to get to work? I probably should have gone the other way. Well, the service road is no better anyway. [sigh] Seriously, this is what I pay these ridiculous taxes for? These politicians have no idea what they're doing. This whole town is a mess. If we had put the house up for sale three years ago, instead of listening to my mother-in-law, we wouldn't even be living here now. Why do we have to live near **them** anyway? It's always about them. What about my family?" And so on, and so on.

Wow. This voice inside your head somehow took the *fact* that there's roadwork being done and created a whole story around it. The only thing that really happened is the construction, but your brain told you what to think, feel, and believe about it. The trap here is that in most situations, we don't even realize that our thoughts and beliefs are surrounding the facts. Instead, to us, our instant interpretations—our mental dialogues—become the facts. They are our reality. If we just look at our lives and what is *actually occurring*, as opposed to what we think about it, then these day-to-day events are not really a problem. They're just things that are happening in our life at that particular time. In other words, these events don't *inherently* mean anything except for the meaning that we give to them. That's why you can have two people sitting in two different cars in the exact same traffic, and the reality of the traffic will occur differently for each person based on the meaning that each gives it.

Can You Control Your Thoughts?

So, we all have this huge collection of thoughts, feelings, opinions, and beliefs about every experience in our lives. This leads us to the million-dollar question: Can you control your thoughts?

You may have answered yes. As a matter of fact, many books have been written that would validate your answer—that you *do* have control over your thoughts.

Well, I have my own theory about this, and it may seem like bad news, but hang in there with me, because it will actually turn into good news. Here goes. *I believe that we have absolutely no control over our thoughts.*

Let me explain.

Where do your thoughts and feelings come from? Well, they come from your learned experiences. Where do your learned experiences come from? They come from your past. Now let me ask you this: Can you go back in time and change your past experiences? Of course you can't. The answer is the same as if I asked whether you could change what you had for dinner yesterday. What you ate is what you ate. Your experiences are your experiences. You can't change them, and it's those very experiences that are the basis for your thoughts and your belief systems about your life. By now, you've created a vast database of thoughts (beliefs, opinions, and expectations) about such things as your defini-tion of success, what will make you happy, what a relationship should look like, what being a good parent is, and the like. I could go on and on. The point is that all the things that you currently think, feel, and believe about all aspects of your life are things that you learned and/or were taught by past experiences.

To show you how little control you have over your thoughts, I'd like you to think of something that really annoys you—one of your pet peeves. I'm going to give you an example of one of mine. As a speaker and coach to companies, I am on airplanes frequently. This pet peeve of mine begins as we pull up to the gate after landing. Although the flight attendant is repeatedly saying, "Please do not get out of your seat until we come to a complete stop," there's always at least one person on every flight who ignores this instruction. As many times as I have experienced this, my internal conversation still goes off like clockwork: "Yep, another human being who insists upon living by his or her own rules, while disre-specting everyone else." My very favorite part comes next. Follow along here with me on the math. Let's say that there are three seats on the left of the plane and three seats on the right of the plane, and the center aisle is about the width of one seat. Even if you're not good at spatial dynam-ics, you can probably figure out that it is *physically impossible* to have six people fit side-by-side in an aisle. Yet, on almost every flight I travel on, passengers try their best to reinvent the laws of physics by jumping up out of their seats and fighting to occupy the same space in the aisle. It's like one of those clown cars in the circus.

Even though I consciously know that all of this is likely to occur, this scenario continues to annoy me each and every time. So let me ask you, what's your pet peeve? What's guaranteed to tick you off every time? Take a moment to picture the situation. You're probably getting agitated just imagining it. Can you now see that we actually have no control over these thoughts and feelings? It's almost as if we are a jukebox, with songs already programmed into our machinery. All someone has to do is stick a dollar in us and press a button, and we automatically play the song associated with that button. When everybody on the plane jumps up to fight for space in the aisle, it's as if somebody pressed "B7" in me, and my mind starts playing the same old song.

So, what can we do about this endless cycle? We're trapped, right? We're doomed! Actually, the answer is elegantly simple. Are you ready? *Do nothing.*

That's right. The first step in the process of designing a life that's worth smiling about is to recognize this simple concept. If your thoughts are automatic, because they were created from your past and you can't change your past, then *stop trying to control your thoughts!* Stop trying to change your thoughts. As a matter of fact, stop trying to change the way you feel. The more you focus on trying to control your thoughts and feelings, or on stopping them, the more they're going to control you. They're going to control you because you're focusing more on them.

The more *attention* you give them, the more they become your *intention*, which means the more they become your reality. You just wind up reinforcing the very things you want to be free of.

This is why some people keep getting into the same type of bad relationships over and over again. Each time it happens, they say, "I've got to stay away from that type of person," but before you know it, there they are, dating the types of people who have proven not to work for them. Why? Because their focus was on that type of relationship, they wind up accepting that type of person into their lives.

Similarly, the reason that so many people struggle with their weight is that they are continually thinking about it. They are constantly focused on being overweight. Studies have shown that the brain can't focus on *not* having something; it can only focus on *having* something. So even if the thought is, "I need to stop eating late at night," the brain is actually focused on "eating late at night."

Let's look at one more example. It's likely that you know some people who are very opinionated about particular topics, such as politics, their bosses, or different social classes. Whenever they have the chance, these people will be overly aggressive in telling anybody who's willing to listen all about their opinions. Have you ever had a conversation with people like this? It seems as if they go on and on about what they think or believe. It's almost as if they can't hear any other point of view, and if you try to express a different perspective, they may follow it up with something like, "Yeah, but," then continue to go on passionately about how you are wrong and how they are right. The next time you engage with people like this, I want you to recognize that they are illustrating what I'm talking about here. They don't have thoughts and opinions; their thoughts and opinions *have them.* As a matter of fact, based on their conditioning, people like this have no choice to do anything other than what they're doing, which is to vehemently tell you what they think. To some extent, however, this is what we all do. We don't have thoughts; thoughts have us. We may not be as obvious as the person we were just talking about, but at some level, we all do the same exact thing. So for right now, at this point in the book, we have to recognize that our thoughts are our thoughts, and they will do what they will do.

Reality Versus Interpretation of Reality

Once we understand that our thoughts will occur, whether we like them or not, we can learn to deal with them effectively. The true power of this concept lies in being able to identify what is *actually* happening in our lives as opposed to how we *interpret* what is happening.

Here's an interesting (and tasty) analogy. If I were baking some cookies, the first ingredient I might use is butter. Think of the butter as the reality of our lives—the facts. While I have that solid hunk of butter, it's easy to deal with. I can measure it, soften it, or melt it if I need to. The next ingredient is the sugar. Think of this as our thoughts and feelings. Once I add sugar to the butter, these two ingredients become something else, and I can no longer deal with them individually. There's no way for me to adjust or remeasure at this point.

It's the same way with our thoughts and feelings. We tend to get into the habit of having them so mixed into our reality that we can no longer separate them.

Now, just as you can't make delicious cookies without both butter *and* sugar, you can't have an awesome life that's worth smiling about without having both the facts *and* your thoughts and feelings. You just have to know how to keep them in the right balance. (More on this as we continue our journey together in future chapters.)

Smile Action Steps

* What have you been avoiding for a long time that would be such a relief and/or would improve the quality of your life if you handled it? It might be looking for a better job, asking for a raise, or doing a project at home.

  _____

  _____

  _____

  _____

_____

_____

_____

❋ What has been the internal conversation you've been having with yourself that's held you back from taking action on this item?

_____

_____

_____

_____

_____

_____

_____

❋ Our thoughts are an ongoing internal conversation that has an opinion about everything. This internal conversation was created while we were growing up. Therefore, we are conditioned based on our past experiences. And, because we can't change our past, we can't change the thoughts that we automatically have (or that have us!). Take a look at something you are always complaining about or upset about. See if you can trace that to a time in your childhood that created that internal conversation.

_____

_____

_____

_____

_____

_____

_____

❋ You might know someone who is very opinionated about nearly everything. I hope that after reading this chapter, you can see that this person is expressing his automatic thinking and that he has very little control over this. The next time you have an interaction with this person, what constructive approach can you take that is a win-win for everyone? (*Note:* We'll take a deeper look at dealing with this effectively in Chapter 16.)

_____

_____

_____

_____

_____

_____

CHAPTER 3

OUR AUTOMATIC THINKING

*Lately in a wreck of a Californian ship, one of the passengers
fastened a belt about him with two hundred pounds of gold in it,
with which he was found afterwards at the bottom. Now, as he
was sinking—had he the gold? or the gold him?*

—John Ruskin, Victorian-era writer

n the previous chapter, we addressed the idea that our thoughts, feelings, opinions, and beliefs are completely beyond our control. Our past experiences have programmed us how to think about people, places, and things, and now, as adults, if something happens to us, we have an immediate thought about that something. So, for example, if a salesperson makes a prospecting call and the person hangs up on him, his thought might be: this isn't going to be easy today.

Now, if something happens to you over and over again, you will start to anticipate it and create a particular way of thinking about it. It's like recognizing a trend or a pattern and making a prediction based on this. It's better than a guess, because it's based on previous knowledge. If you have a series of numbers, for instance, you can look for a pattern and then make an educated guess as to what number would come next. If I gave you the numbers 2, 4, 6, and 8, you would probably predict that the next number would be 10, based on your existing knowledge of even numbers. You recognized a pattern, and your brain instantly filled in the next result. We do the same thing in all areas of our lives.

"Automatic Thinking"

If you wake up in the morning and it's overcast and windy, you don't need a meteorologist's opinion to tell you that it may rain later. You can predict this yourself, based on your own experience. As you go out the door, you grab an umbrella. Your prediction actually influenced your action. The question here is, "Is it certain that there will be rain?" Of course not. There are too many variables involved that could change the outcome. Now, in this case, it's not a big deal that you carried an umbrella when it wasn't needed, but let's take a look at what happens when we have this type of predictable thinking in other areas that have a bigger impact on the quality of our lives.

Let's say you work in an environment in which there are weekly office meetings, and there is one member of the group (let's call him Bob) who, more often than not, shows up 10 minutes late. Based on this pattern, you might draw the conclusion that Bob is irresponsible, or even disrespectful. One morning, you're assigned to a big project, and Bob is made a member of your team. Before you even start on this project, I bet you're going to have some thoughts about working with him. You might even predict what it's going to be like dealing with Bob and/or how the project is going to turn out. Take a minute right now and stop reading. Listen to the thoughts you would have about working with Bob on this project.

Now, here's the problem. Your mind can do what it does and generate a number of thoughts ("This is going to be a nightmare. I'm going to have to pull both my weight and his. I know I can't trust Bob to do his part," and so on), creating automatic thinking about Bob. (By the way, some synonyms for "automatic" include "unthinking," "mindless," and "programmed." So, you see, it's truly beyond our control!)

As a result, before the project even begins, you have already predicted what's going to happen. You'll begin to work with Bob, but all your interactions with him will be biased because of the preconceptions you have about him. Now let me ask you: do you think this automatic thinking is going to influence your working relationship with Bob? I would bet that not only will your automatic thinking influence how you work with him, but it is actually going to *create* the results that you think are going to happen. In other words, your thoughts about the situation will cause you to act in a certain way—for example, perhaps you duplicate Bob's work on the assignment because you don't trust what he says, leading him to grow angry and actively try to undermine your efforts. Thus, your actions have led to the result that you predicted in the first place. This is a wonderful example of your thoughts creating a self-fulfilling prophecy: ("Bob is a screw-up. . . . I can't work with him. . . . I'll do all the work because he is untrustworthy. . . . Now he is fighting me at every step. . . . Our project is in jeopardy. . . . See, I told you this would never work!")

Let's look at another example. Say you have a fight with your spouse about how he doesn't take out the garbage as often as he used to. If you have this fight two or three times, before you know it, you start to get annoyed before you're even out of bed, because you're assuming that he didn't take the garbage out the night before. You are literally waking up into this automatic thinking.

This, in turn, can start a fight first thing in the morning, which may then result in your spouse *purposely* not taking out the garbage the following night and therefore validating your automatic thinking.

Similarly, have you ever woken up in a bad mood? There's a good chance that you were experiencing an automatic thought about something or someone. But the "funny" (or actually sad) thing is that nothing has even happened yet for you to be annoyed at. Yet your preprogrammed, involuntary mind has been hard at work, setting the tone for your upcoming day.

So, how do we deal with this issue? Well, the first thing to remember, just as we discussed in the previous chapter, is that there is no miracle cure. The key to dealing with automatic thinking is to *know* that it will happen and *accept* it as part of being human. You see, your brain wants to make sense of the things that happen in your life, and it is comfortable when it sees a pattern that it can neatly categorize. We're naturally more secure with things that we know or believe—even if these things are negative—than we are when we are living a life full of unknown (and therefore uncomfortable) possibilities.

The second thing to do is to simply make a statement before you take any action. The simple statement: "Oh, there goes my automatic thinking again" will help you take a step back. It will allow you to separate fact from fiction, and you will see things a little more clearly.

A good clue to look for when you're trying to recognize automatic thinking is whether you have a strong emotion concerning a particular thought, person, or situation. If you "dread" the holidays, that's automatic thinking at work. It could be the result of past experiences with your family, or it could be the anticipation of the credit card bills in January. Whatever it is, these are the experiences that you *already know* from your past that are now shaping the way you view something that hasn't happened yet. There's no certainty that the coming holiday season will be something negative for you, but you're already putting yourself in the frame of mind that it will be. It's very important that you are aware of this, because if you don't recognize when automatic thinking is occurring, you will continue to take actions based on your past experiences. Worst of all, you'll leave no room for positive opportunities to emerge.

Your Automatic Thoughts Kill Off Possibility

Last summer, while my son, Michael, and I were visiting my Uncle Jack down in Florida, we drove to get something to eat. As I was sitting at the drive-through window, I happened to notice a trail of ants walking up and down the concrete wall. They were busy, marching along in their formation, obviously doing something that was important in their ant world. As I stared at them, I started to wonder what they "thought" of their world. Did they ever venture off of this wall? Did they know that anyplace else existed beyond this building—that just across the parking lot were trees and grass, then another building, and so on?

I sat there thinking, "If I were one of these ants, and I didn't know any better, I might think that this wall was the entire world." Sometimes, we can have this type of small, nearsighted thinking. As we go through our lives, we have to remember the possibility that there is much more to our world than just that little patch of concrete that we're on at the time.

Our lives can expand only to the degree that we allow our minds to expand. If you're walking through your life telling yourself, "This is all there is," I can assure you that will become true for you. Have you ever heard the story about the two friends who were out fishing? One of the two noticed something very interesting about the way the other one was choosing which fish he would keep, so he asked him about it. "Why is it that every time you catch a really big fish, you throw it back, but when you catch the small ones, you keep them?" His friend answered, "My frying pan is too small for those big fish."

Imagine how many big fish you're throwing away because you view your life as a small frying pan. How many opportunities are you letting pass by? How many awesome ideas are you telling yourself could never happen? How many exciting journeys are you not taking? How many potentially amazing relationships are you never even attempting to start? A life full of limiting thinking is not a life that's worth smiling about. More likely, it's a path to a life of unrealized potential and regret.

At the end of this chapter, you'll have a chance to write down and take a look at where you might be caught in your own limiting thinking. I think you may be surprised at how powerful your thoughts are at dismissing some of the ideas, goals, or dreams that you would like to achieve. Let's say, for example, that you want to be the top salesperson in your office next month. Got that? Really picture it. Now, was there another voice creeping up inside of you, saying, "Well, nobody ever beats so-and-so"? It's *that* automatic—you don't even realize it's happening.

When you write your list later, you may not write something as daunting as creating a molecular transportation device like in Star Trek, but if that's one of your goals, make sure you write it down! History has taught us that many people have accomplished things that were first considered out of this world. As a matter of fact, not only were they successfully brought into reality, but they have actually been surpassed by even more "unbelievable" advances. My point here is to illustrate to you just how easily our minds will default to *limiting* thinking.

Allowing our minds to dictate the things we believe we can do will always hold us back from our true potential.

Smile Action Steps

* Let's take a look at some automatic thinking you may have in certain areas of your life. If I were to ask you what your thoughts are right now about your finances, what would you say? On the left side of the chart that follows are several areas of your life. Next to each of them, I would like you to write a statement that represents the thoughts you have about that relationship or area.

Life Category	Automatic Thinking
Weight/health	
Your spouse or significant other	
Money	
A friend (name them)	
A parent	
A business colleague/office associate	

* OK, be honest. Do your thoughts about each of these areas correlate with the way that area of your life is going right now? In other words, if you wrote something positive in a given area, is that part of your life working pretty well? Or if you wrote something negative, are you having problems in that area of your life? Let me suggest something: *the results we have in our lives are a result of what we think, not the other way around.*

I'd like you to take a moment and examine how you may be holding on to limiting thinking right now. The possibility chart that follows gives a few key areas of your life, and I want you to think of something in each area that would really cause you to smile. This can be a major accomplishment or a small goal— just be sure that it's something that would make you happy.

In the area of Children, for example: it may be "to have a child" (major), but it can also be as simple as "to eat dinner with my children at least four times a week." Whatever it is, just go with it!

Life Area	If Anything Were Possible I Would...
CAREER	
FINANCES	
SIGNIFICANT OTHER	
CHILDREN	
HEALTH	
FAMILY/FRIENDS	
LEISURE	
FAITH	

❋ Now that you've written some things down, I'd like you to listen
   to the voice in your head and what it's telling you. I bet there
   are more than a few places where it's saying things like:

   ❋ "That's nice, but it's just not gonna happen."
   ❋ "Get that promotion or start that business? I'm way too
      young/old."
   ❋ "Have zero debt? I don't believe it when I hear people say
      they have none; they must be lying."
   ❋ "Sell my home and move to a warmer climate? No way my
      family would go for that."
   ❋ "Have all of my siblings talking to one another? My family is
      way too dysfunctional."
   ❋ "I'll never make it home in time to have dinner with my kids
      all those nights."

In the next chapter, we're going to look at how to move beyond our
automatic, limiting thoughts and start to create mini-miracles in our
life. When you learn to embrace *possibility thinking* (more on this later)
rather than *automatic thinking*, your whole world will expand exponen-
tially. You'll no longer be one of those ants on that concrete wall, certain
that where you are *now* is the only place to be. You have to allow yourself
to envision what could be on the other side of that parking lot, beyond
those trees. Believe me, there's grass over there. You just haven't figured
out how to get there yet.

CHAPTER 4

HOW TO MOVE BEYOND YOUR AUTOMATIC THINKING

Concerning all acts of initiative (and creation), there is one elementary truth the ignorance of which kills countless ideas and splendid plans: that the moment one definitely commits one-self, then Providence moves too.

—W. H. Murray, *The Scottish Himalayan Expedition* (1951)

pollo 13 was the seventh manned mission in the American Apollo space program, and the third that was intended to land on the Moon. I say intended, since it never actually landed there. Because of a series of horrible malfunctions, the crew had to turn around and come back to Earth. One of the major challenges the mission faced involved something called the air scrubbers. These were the devices that took carbon dioxide out of the capsule, "scrubbed" it clean, and put clean oxygen back into the capsule. Well, the scrubber in the Command Module was damaged, which meant that the crew members would suffocate before they were able to make it home. The solution, it seemed, was to connect the scrubber from the Lunar Module to the Command Module. The problem was that the cartridge in the Command Module was square and the Lunar Module device was round. The crew literally had to figure out how to take a square item and fit it into a round hole, all while in the midst of outer space with limited supplies and dwindling oxygen!

Commitment

In Ron Howard's brilliant film about this mission, *Apollo 13*, my favorite scene is when the Lead Flight Director, Gene Kranz, is brainstorming with Mission Control department heads about how to fix this and the other problems they have to contend with. There were many conversations going on about what could be done, why a particular option had never been tested before, why devices were designed this way, and so on. If you look at that brainstorming session in the movie, there were a lot of people who were operating from their thoughts and feelings regarding why this was a doomed mission and these men were going to die in space.

Let's take what happened in the movie and put it into a diagram. You'll see that we have our "box," which is our thoughts, feelings, and opinions—and then there is what happens outside the box, where life actually occurs. In this example, what happened was that there was an explosion that set off a whole chain of events. That's a fact. Now, the entire team, as depicted in the movie, started to share its concerns. These sounded like, "This can't be done; the equipment wasn't built this way; it's never been tried before," and the like.

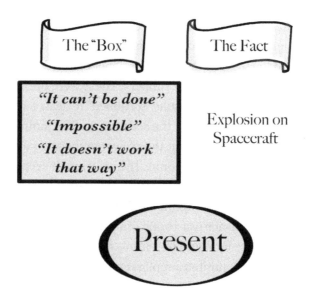

Now, as we said earlier, our automatic thoughts were created from our past experiences. They are made up of things that were specifically taught to us, and other things that we interpreted and absorbed while we were growing up. Therefore, we can make a strong assertion that every time we listen to our automatic thoughts and take action based on them, we're living from our past—or, to put it another way, we're bringing our past into our present situation. Living this way doesn't give us access to what's possible in our future. So, if we were to continue drawing this model, it would look something like the figure that follows.

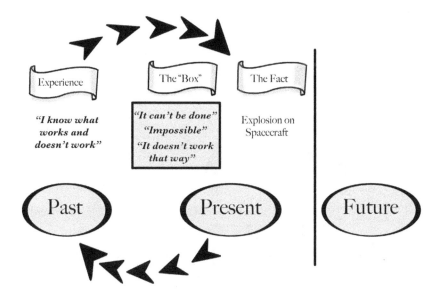

We can use this diagram to illustrate a lot of aspects of our life. As we noted in Chapter 2, there are people who keep getting into the same types of bad relationships over and over again, and while every time they say they're not going to repeat the same mistakes, they continue to do so. They keep living based on their past experiences, bringing negative thoughts and behavior patterns from those experiences into the present, and creating results similar to those they have had previously. Another example might be people who are constantly having troubles at their job, or they seem to get a new job every six months, or they don't get the raise and somebody gets promoted over them, and so on. If you have a persistent problem that seems to keep occurring in your life, it's probably caused by your bringing experiences from your past into your present situation. So, how do we break that cycle? Let's go back to our movie, *Apollo 13*.

During the brainstorming session, when everyone was sharing their opinion about why these men were going to die in space, Gene Kranz had had enough, and this is when he makes his brilliant, now famous, declaration to the team: ***"Failure is not an option."***

What Kranz was telling the people on his team was that he expected them to live from their *commitment* to getting these guys home safely. They were not to let their thoughts, feelings, and concerns get in the way. He was determined to get those men home safely, even when the circumstances, from most perspectives, dictated that they would soon be dead.

Now, if we were to complete our diagram, it would look something like the one shown here.

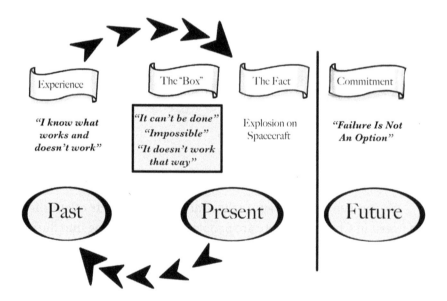

If we pay too much attention to our thoughts, and we take action based on them (or on how we feel or what we believe), we are actually taking our past and bringing it into our future, killing off new possibilities. Either we are living from what we are really committed to, or we are living from our past. It's one or the other. That is, either you are making a conscious choice to take actions based on something that you're committed to, leading toward a desired goal or next level, or you are acting based on automatic thoughts that come from your past experiences. Which do you think is more powerful?

If you look at any area in your life where you created amazing results, it's because you were committed to achieving something bigger than the temporary circumstances would seem to allow. Like Gene Kranz, you were behaving as if "failure was *not* an option."

Conviction

Commitment coupled with a firm belief in what you've set out to achieve is what I mean by *conviction*. Conviction is like the icing on the cake of commitment, helping us push past the pain and through negative internal monologues such as "I don't want to do it." *Webster's Dictionary* also adds to the definition "a strong persuasion." Simply put, if you are to have conviction, you must believe, deep in your core, in the thing that you are committed to.

Imagine that you're in a large room with a ceiling height of 15 feet, and that there's a big brick wall running down the middle of the room from end to end. The wall is 12 feet high, and there is no door or side entrance. The only way you can get to the other side of this 12-foot wall is by climbing over it. You have nothing at your disposal to help you: no ladder, cables, or rope. It's just you and the wall. Now, let's say that by accident, your child or grandchild finds himself trapped on the other side of this brick wall. Are you going to find a way over that wall? Chances are you will do whatever it takes to reach him. Why? Not just because you're committed, but because you have conviction. You have the belief that you can and *must* do *whatever it takes* to succeed in saving your loved one. You will find a way, no question about it.

Sometimes conviction springs from a situation in which people are so fed up with what's happening that they feel a sense of desperation, as if they have no other choice but to act. When harnessed correctly, this can be a good thing. Here are two historical examples in which this "do whatever it takes" mentality produced positive results.

Many years ago, there was a group of people who were disenchanted with the conditions in which they lived. They were tired of a government that did not represent them, bullied them, and suppressed what they believed to be their God-given rights as human beings. They made a commitment, and they had the conviction to bring about a new future—a reality that provided them with what they deserved. In 1776, the United States of America was created by a group of people who were fed up and weren't going to take it anymore. They took a stand for something in which they passionately believed.

In our more recent history, in 1969, Fred Rogers (of the famed PBS show *Mister Rogers' Neighborhood*) appeared before the U.S. Senate Subcommittee on Communications.[1] His *commitment* was to support funding for PBS and the Corporation for Public Broadcasting in response to significant cuts proposed by President Nixon. What was in jeopardy was a $20 million grant. The committee had pretty much decided to cut the funding, but the Senate nonetheless allowed Rogers' input, more as a formality than with the expectation that his words would make a difference. Mr. Rogers didn't get emotional or worked up over it; he just calmly sat down to have a heart-to-heart with the Senate about feelings and imagination. Here's just a portion of what he said:

We deal with such things as the inner drama of childhood. We don't need to bop someone over the head to make drama over a scene; we deal with such things as getting a haircut or the feelings about brothers and sisters. . . . I give an expression of care every day to each child.

Rogers was clear and focused. If you watch the actual hearing, you can see his personal passion and the *conviction* that he had concerning his cause. Before Rogers spoke, Senator John Pastore, who was head of the committee, had seemed impatient, even gently making fun of Rogers and his children's programming for the first couple of minutes. But by the end, after Fred Rogers shared the lyrics of a song that he had written about children's feelings, here's what John Pastore had to say: "I'm supposed to be a pretty tough guy and this is the first time I've had goosebumps for the last two days . . . looks like you just earned the $20 million." When you have an unwavering commitment to a cause, outcome, or goal, as Fred Rogers did, that is the true meaning of conviction. (I highly encourage you to watch this video. You can find the URL in the endnotes.)

Conviction is not just seen in a historical context. Successful companies these days also see the value of tapping into the personal convictions of their workers. Google, for example, has a "20 percent policy" that requires employees to earmark a fifth of their office time for pursuing a project that they're personally passionate about and have the conviction to achieve.[2] This practice has brought about such innovative products as Gmail and Google Earth's flight simulator software. But most important, it demonstrates the power of unleashing the creativity and drive that is within us all. Our task is to learn how to access this creativity and drive and channel it productively.

Being Versus Doing

To bring about the result you desire, your conviction has to translate into action. And your entire being, like that of Mr. Rogers, has to radiate your commitment.

In 1994, I was watching the Winter Olympics and one of my favorite competitions, downhill skiing. Markus Wasmeier from Germany won the men's gold medal. Immediately following his performance, a reporter asked, *"How were you feeling going into the race?"* I loved what he said so much that I furiously jotted down notes to try to capture the essence of his answer. Here's a summary of his response:

> *The conditions for me to win were right. I felt no stress or pressure—no anxiety, which is my biggest adversary. When you feel too much or think too much, then you're not skiing, you're thinking—the continuous mind is too slow. If I'm thinking about the next marker, I know I'm losing. I know I've done good when I get to the bottom of the hill and all I remember is the top.*

Consider that for a moment. Being in action is what will help you overcome the automatic thoughts that try to derail you or hold you back. I want you to imagine a point in your life when you had a tremendous amount to do in a short period of time. As a matter of fact, if you looked at how much you had to accomplish in the amount of time that you were given, it seemed impossible. For example, you could have been getting ready for a holiday event. You had to shop *and* clean *and* wrap presents. Then you had to set the table *and* cook the 47 different recipes that had sounded like a good idea when you were planning the menu last month.

Now let me ask you this question: While you were doing all these things, what *wasn't* there for you? I'll tell you what wasn't there: your thoughts, feelings, beliefs, and opinions. The only thing that showed up was the action. You didn't have time to question yourself. You didn't have time to have an opinion. The only thing you could do was act.

Think back to other times when you've been "in the zone." When you're in the middle of accomplishing great things, all of a sudden you'll shake your head and say, "Where has the time gone?" It's as if the conscious *you* wasn't even there. It's at those times that you were *being your commitment.* This is the distinction of *being* versus *doing.*

When my son was younger I forced him to take piano lessons, like any good parent does. (What? They don't?) Well, at least I didn't make him suffer alone. I also took the lessons with him. After doing this for a year, he was ready to pack his bags and leave me at the tender age of 10! It was during this time that I learned something very important about being versus doing. Once I learned to read the music and got the basics down, I did much better when I didn't think too much. Just as the gold medalist said, "The continuous mind is too slow"; when you are playing the piano, you cannot *do* the song, you have to *be* the music. Similarly, if a ballerina starts to look at her feet and ask herself, "Am I doing this correctly?" or, "Am I moving my feet the right way?" that's when she messes up. You can't *do* ballet; you must *be* the dance.

Unfold What Already Is

How would you feel if I told you that everything you want already exists? What if the things that you envision for yourself and your life are already here, waiting for you? What if these possibilities are realities, just around the corner, and all you have to do is take the right actions to bring them into existence?

Sounds a little metaphysical, right? Well, it is. But stick with me; it's worth it.

I would like you to consider this quote from Martin Heidegger:

> *We are still far from pondering the essence of action decisively enough. We view action only as causing an effect. The actuality of the effect is valued according to its utility. But the essence of action is accomplishment. To accomplish means to unfold something into the fullness of its essence, to lead it forth into this fullness. Therefore only what already is can really be accomplished.*

This concept is the most inspiring and empowering one that comes from opening yourself up to possibility. When you're looking at your goals and making a commitment to them, instead of perceiving them as things that don't exist and that you have to somehow create (which can feel overwhelming at times), I'd like you to imagine that they are already here—you just can't see them yet. You don't have to create something out of nothing; you just have to figure out how to bring your goals into reality.

Have you ever heard the saying, "When the student is ready, the teacher appears"? Said another way, "Your reward will materialize when you are open to receiving it" or "when you are committed to achieving it." How often has this happened to you at work? Once you decide that you want to accomplish something—such as being selected for a certain committee or getting a promotion—you "suddenly" discover resources that can help you get there. It could be that the guy in the office down the hall is a whiz at creating dynamic presentations like the type you'll need in order to impress your boss. Until you decided that you needed to be able to do a presentation like this to move forward in your career, you never bothered to speak with him. However, he was right there all along!

Think about it. What if you and I are all sculptors and we've been presented with a giant block of marble, within which is our perfect life—our ideal relationships, family, finances, career, health, you name it. It's all in there. It already exists, but it's waiting for us to chisel it to the surface. We need to commit to the result we want with conviction and determination and take action to "reveal" what is rightfully ours!

Here's a fascinating example of this concept. One of my favorite shows when I was growing up was Gene Roddenberry's television series *Star Trek*. Most people who watched this show back in the 1960s and 1970s probably thought that it was science fiction and make-believe. Let me point out some really interesting facts about that show, however—facts that reveal how the writers of the program created a new reality that eventually became true in the "real world" that we all live in.

* The characters had a device called a "communicator" that gave the crew the ability to talk to each other wirelessly. If you look at this communicator, it looks very much like the Motorola flip phone. So, in the 1960s the program was showing cellular phones, long before cellular service was even on the drawing board. (In fact, the people watching the program at the time were using rotary-dial phones! For those who are too young, rotary phones actually had a dial and no push buttons. How primitive!)

- Lieutenant Uhura was the communications officer. She sat on the bridge at the switchboard, patching communications from ship to ship. When this show was filmed, real-life operators were using headsets, but on the Starship *Enterprise*, Lieutenant Uhura used what appeared to be a Bluetooth device in her ear.
- Mr. Spock, played by Leonard Nimoy, was the science officer on the *Enterprise*. Whenever he needed to access data, he used something that looked exactly like a 3 × 5 floppy disk, which we all started to use when the personal computer came out nearly 20 years later.
- Captain Kirk never needed a pen or paper; he wrote on a digital pad. Watch the show and you'll see them using something that looks like an iPad or any other touch-screen tablet.

Like I said, this was my favorite show, so I could go on and on about this, but those are just a few examples. Now, here's my question: Did cell phones, personal computers, and tablets already exist in the 1960s? Yes, they did—we just hadn't brought them into actual existence yet. The concepts were certainly there; they just needed time, effort, and commitment to be nurtured into reality.

Smile Action Steps

- There is a distinction, a separation, between the reality of our lives and what we think and feel about our lives. When something happens, that event is separate from what we think, feel, and believe *about* what happened. When we separate what happens from what we think, feel, and believe, we see that the thing that happened doesn't really "mean" anything. The only meaning is the meaning that we give it. So, essentially, life as it happens—the whole thing—really doesn't mean anything except for the meaning that we give it. What challenge or issue are you facing right now? Can you separate the event from the meaning you are placing on it? Write it as two separate sentences—for example, the first would be, "Here is the event I am having a challenge with:," and the second would be, "And here are all my thoughts, feelings, and beliefs about it."

_____

_____

_____

_____

_____

_____

_____

❋ Have you ever had something you were working toward where you had a total conviction and belief that it was going to work out? Can you think of a time in your life where "failure was not an option"? Record that moment here:

_____

_____

_____

_____

_____

_____

_____

❋ Think of a time when you had to do *so many* tasks in a short period of time, and you successfully accomplished them. Record that moment now.

_____

_____

_____

_____

_____

_____

_____

* As an exercise to get you to start thinking from a place of possibility, write down a few scientific advancements you can think
of that are possible in the future.

_____

_____

_____

_____

_____

_____

_____

CHAPTER 5

DESIGNING YOUR
NEXT LEVEL

When your memories outweigh your dreams,
that's when you become old.

—Bill Clinton, 42nd U.S. president

When you look at your life, there probably have been moments that you consider to have been truly life-altering—those that permanently changed who you are. For example, getting married would qualify. The same goes for having a child, landing your first job, and graduating from college. These experiences are not merely goals, but what I call the Next Level. Most goals are specific things that you want to achieve or obtain, like a new car, a rise in your income, finishing a project, and so on. Goals are important to have and achieve, but a *Next Level* changes your entire life.

Let me ask you a question: Are you a different person today from the person you were seven years ago? What about ten years ago? Chances are that if you look back, you will see those moments that totally changed you as a person. Think about that for a second.

I would like you to make a list of four life-altering moments—major accomplishments that have created totally new meaning in your life.

1. _____

2. _____

3. _____

4. _____

These life-altering events that have had a serious impact on your quality of life are what I call Next Level events.

A Next Level event is personal and specific to your life. Such events will be different for everyone. Let me give you some examples:

* For a newlywed, it may be to purchase your first home or to have a child.
* If you're a parent, it may be for all of your children to graduate from college.
* In the business world, it may be to reach a certain position, or maybe to start your own business.
* For an athlete, it might be to improve your "numbers."

Do What You Love

The most important element of a Next Level event is that it has to be something that makes your heart sing. It's something that you *love* to do; it's a job that you would take even if you didn't get paid for doing it. It's the thing that wakes you up in the morning before the alarm clock even goes off, because you're so energized by the thought of the day ahead. Some of us start off our day more tired than we were when we went to bed because we're not moving toward a Next Level. We are waking up to an alarm clock rather than an exciting vision for our lives. A life that is spent just "going through the motions" is not a life that's worth smiling about.

Here's something about myself that's a perfect example of this topic. I've always been what you would call a "night person." Unless I'm on the road and have to get up early to deliver a seminar, I find that I'm more focused and productive at night. But check this out: once I began writing this book, although I was still keeping my late schedule at night, I was waking up one to two hours earlier in the morning. The first thing on my mind was to get all the new ideas out of my head and onto the computer. I was so excited about what I had to say that I couldn't wait to start working. When you do something that you enjoy, the actual work is the reward. The success and money will come later.

Do you have something in your life that's similar to this? Something that excites you, energizes you, and makes you smile just thinking about it? Keep this question in the back of your head as we continue. Toward the end of this chapter, I'll give you some exercises to help shape your thoughts and bring your Next Level closer to reality.

First, I want to tell you about a woman named Rachael Lust from Marion, Ohio. This young lady is a "hooper." For those of you who don't know what that is (I didn't), she does hula hooping for fitness, dance, and so on. I came to know of her after clicking on a random video link in my Facebook news feed, and I was just blown away. First of all, I had no idea that hula hooping was making this huge comeback! So here's this girl, videotaping herself in her kitchen, doing these incredible moves to the song "Thrift Shop" by Macklemore and Ryan Lewis. At the time, I had just gotten the idea of interviewing people who are living a life worth smiling about, and I had a hunch that she was one. So, I messaged her, telling her my idea, and we set up a phone interview.

"So, how long have you been doing this?" I asked her.

"I've been doing it about 20 months now," she replied.

"How often do you practice, and for how long?" I inquired.

"One to two hours every day," she said.

When I asked her if she ever got up in the morning and just didn't feel like practicing, she answered, "Not really. If there are those rare times, I don't push myself, because I don't want this to be something I *have* to do. Honestly, I just do it because I love doing it."

Here's the punch line to Rachael's story: she now has her own You-Tube channel with more than 8,500 subscribers and more than 1.6 million views (as of this writing), she is making and selling her own customized hula hoops on Etsy, she is teaching hooping classes, and she has been asked to appear on her local television news channel.

If you visit Rachael's YouTube channel (I highly encourage you to), make sure you pay attention to the *About* section. Some users fill this section with tons of descriptive content, telling subscribers who they are, what they represent, why they started making videos, blah blah blah. Rachael's has only two simple sentences, but they epitomize what I mean by Next Level: "First started hooping July 2011. Life hasn't been the same since."

Now, *that's* what I'm talking about! Your Next Level must be something that's worth smiling about, something that you love doing. It should inspire you so much that you will push past internal thoughts of defeat that would stop most people. Notice that Rachael didn't set out to build a

Next Level or accomplish anything specific through her hooping. She was just following her heart. Even so, her efforts have resulted in many opportunities—business and otherwise—that she can now pursue. In your case, since you are reading this book and clearly have an interest in proactively designing your life, I'm suggesting that you consciously incorporate doing what you love into your Next Level planning process.

Envision It

There's a story I heard about Roy Disney and the opening of Epcot Center at Disney World in Orlando, Florida. On the opening day, a newspaper reporter approached Roy and said to him, "This must be a bittersweet day for you." Roy asked, "What do you mean?" The reporter answered, "Well, it's great that this new park is being opened, and it looks fabulous, but it's a shame that Walt didn't live to see it." To that, Roy replied, "My brother did see it; that's why we're standing here today."

The ability to clearly "see" something that hasn't yet materialized is part of the path to your Next Level. You must be able to visualize whatever it is that you want in the future. If you allow your mind to see the bigger picture, it will subconsciously begin to work on achieving it.

If you were to ask people who are good at doing jigsaw puzzles (I'm horrible at them), "What's the most important piece of the puzzle?" you would get different answers. Some might say that it's one of the corner pieces, while others would say that it's the center piece. Now, the real pros will tell you that the most important piece of the jigsaw puzzle is the cover of the box, because that shows you what the end result should look like! From there, your brain starts to look at each and every piece in the context of how to complete that picture. The same is true for your life.

Smile Action Steps: Design Your Next Level

So, let's get hands-on. How do you figure out your Next Level? What makes you smile? First, you brainstorm. When you do this, you must be unreasonable. Don't edit yourself. Write down anything that comes to mind. Let it flow. This process helps you to break away from all your thinking about what you can and cannot do.

1. When I was growing up, I dreamed of being

   _____

   _____

   _____

   _____.

2. If I were in a contest for accomplishing something, I would win first place for

   _____

   _____

   _____

   _____.

3. The one positive thing about me that I secretly love and that no one knows about me is

   _____

   _____

   _____

   _____.

4. If I were to create my own business, and if I had all of my financial needs met, that business would be

   _____

   _____

   _____

   _____.

5. If I work for a company and I could have any position in that company, it would be

_____

_____

_____

_____.

6. The one thing I would *really* love to learn is

_____

_____

_____

_____.

7. If I had free time to myself this week, away from work and the family, I would be

_____

_____

_____

_____.

8. My friends think I am really good at

_____

_____

_____

_____.

9. The thing I would love to do as a hobby is

_____

_____

_____

_____.

10. The thing that makes me smile the most is when

_____

_____

_____

_____.

11. The things I am really good at, in my personal life or in business, are

_____

_____

_____

_____.

12. The thing that I would really like to accomplish, but that I have been putting off, is

_____

_____

_____

_____.

13. The skills that come to me with very little thought or effort (for example, helping others, solving problems, or doing something with my hands) are

_____

_____

_____

_____.

14. The job I would do (even if I wasn't paid for it) because I would enjoy it so much is

_____

_____

_____

_____.

15. When I take the time to read, the subjects I like to read about the most are

_____

_____

_____

_____.

16. When I volunteer, I really enjoy

_____

_____

_____

_____.

17. Of all the things that I do on a weekly basis, the activities that I have the most fun doing are

_____

_____

_____

_____.

18. My favorite subject in college or high school was

_____

_____

_____

_____.

19. I literally lose myself and lose track of time when I am

_____

_____

_____

_____.

20. If I had free time on my hands, I would

_____

_____

_____

_____.

21. Now, I would like you to make a list of the careers of some of your closest friends and family members. Is there anything that grabs your interest?

_____

_____

_____

_____.

For the next step in this process, here is a list of suggestions. These are totally random. I want you to look at these possibilities and see whether any of them speaks to your heart. Perhaps the specific item that I have listed may not inspire you exactly the way I wrote it, but it may bring up some other ideas that might work for you.

* Reach my goal weight.
* Make working out a regular part of my daily routine.
* Meet a "special someone" to spend time with.
* Close 100 sales in a year for my company.
* Get a college degree in a subject I've always been interested in.
* Sell my house and move to someplace I've always dreamed of.
* Get a major promotion at my company.
* Learn to speak another language.
* Become proficient at playing an instrument.
* Make an important speech to a large audience.
* Make a music video.
* Run a marathon.
* Write a book and get it published.

Now, for the last phase, I would like you to look at everything that you wrote previously and the list of items that I gave you, and pick the top five things that you would like to commit to accomplishing in your life. Write them here and begin to think about how you will move forward to accomplish them. (More on this in the next chapter!)

1. _____

2. _____

3. _____

4. _____

5. _____

As you began to design your Next Level, you should have gotten excited about the possibility of what your life can be used for—a purpose bigger than who you are that contributes not only to the quality of your life, but to the lives of others as well. If you haven't, go back and rework this exercise before you read the next chapter, because we are about to start working on implementing a plan to bring your Next Level into reality.

CHAPTER 6

HOW TO ACHIEVE YOUR NEXT LEVEL

Many persons have a wrong idea of what constitutes true happiness. It is not attained through self-gratification but through fidelity to a worthy purpose.

—Joseph Addison, seventeenth–eighteenth-century author and politician

So now that you have your Next Level vision, it's important that you have a plan for how you're going to get there. You see, in order for you to achieve this "new you," you can't keep doing the same things that you've been doing because if you do, you'll simply get the same results you've been getting. So having a vision and a dream of a Next Level is not enough. You must take the *actions* necessary to facilitate bringing this new reality into the present.

Let's say you have a vision of having a huge crop of flowers in your backyard. I mean huge—like an acre. So you sit on your back deck thinking about it, dreaming about it, and envisioning it. You call all your friends and talk about what the crop is going to look like. Now, is all that thinking, dreaming, and talking going to produce flowers for you? I hope you said no. In order to create this beautiful acre, you actually have to get up from your chair, walk off the deck, and get dirty.

Some of the required tasks might include researching different types of flowers, seeds, fertilizer, planting techniques, watering techniques, and how to deal with weeds. If you take no action, then you'll get no results. And if you take some action only some of the time, you'll get poor results at best.

It's easy to not follow through on our plans because we usually do what we *feel* like doing instead of what we *should* be doing. So let me share with you some suggestions that I think will really help you to stay *focused* on the actions you need to take if you are to bring your Next Level into reality.

The steps that follow are not just things that I made up to put in this book—I actually use them myself! During the process of writing this book, I wanted to lose 25 pounds in 5 months. It was hard, but I did it. Many of these steps helped me along the way. Here's what I did, and what I recommend to you if you want to produce amazing results in your life.

Action Steps to Reach Your Next Level

There are a number of action steps that you can take to reach your Next Level.

Create a Vision Board

If you have a child who has gone to grammar school, or if you can remember what it was like when you were a child yourself, it's possible that you or your child created some kind of collage on a poster board to try to illustrate a concept. A vision board consists of visual representations that you gather from the Internet, from magazines, or from newspaper clippings. You simply cut or print them out and paste them on a poster board to help illustrate the Next Level that you're committed to accomplishing. Then you place the vision board in a prominent location in your home or office, so that you can look at it frequently. Your mind will subconsciously seek out and create whatever you are focused on the most. This simple step has proven to be a powerful technique for many of my students when they are trying to create change in their lives.

Write It Down

Take a 3 × 5 index card and write the statement: "This is the new life that I am committed to bringing into my reality." Then list the Next Level items that you wrote down in the previous chapter. Carry this card with you, and take it out whenever you have a free moment. Give it a read. I like to put the statement on an index card, since it makes it so much more tangible for me, but feel free to post it on the wallpaper on your phone or to send it to yourself as a calendar reminder as well. Just make sure you look at the statement every day.

Make Your Commitment Public

During the time period in which I had committed to losing the 25 pounds, I was teaching a six-month sales training program. I was asking these salespeople to commit to activities that would stretch them, and to do things that they really didn't want to do. I told them that I would do the same. So I made a public commitment to them that I would lose 25 pounds by the last class. The more people you declare your commitment to, the harder it is for you to back out. You see, one of the things that drives human beings is that we don't like to look bad in front of others. (That's probably why we spend so much time getting ready in the morning.) So obviously we don't want to tell everybody we know that we don't meet our goals and keep our promises. And, with today's technology and social media, it is much easier to make our promises very public.

Be Held Accountable

When I met with the class each month, I had a scale in the room, and at the beginning of each class, I weighed myself in front of the whole group so that people could see whether I was getting closer to my Next Level. Honestly, just before I got on the scale each month, I was afraid that the number would have gone up, but fortunately, each month I showed progress. Hopefully, you have a close friend or loved one who will help you stay focused on creating the new habits you need if you are to get to your Next Level. Tell this person your specific goal and why it is so important to you to have this habit become a routine in your life. Periodically give her updates and share some of your challenges so that she can help you push past those barriers.

Remove Obstacles; Create a Habit

When I committed to losing 25 pounds, I knew I had to make it easy to start eating in a healthier way. So I had to remove all the sugary items from the house. (Although my 17-year-old son didn't like this part, he was also committed to helping me reach my goal, so he got on board.) The next step was to decide on the plan I was going to use to lose the weight. There are a lot of great diet programs out there, and I think most of the better ones work, as long as you stick to the plan. The one I decided to use was a diet that had all the meals except one already made for me. That one, I prepared on my own. This setup was a huge help. I didn't have to agonize about shopping, cooking, reading charts, weighing food, and the like throughout the day. All I had to do was open a package and follow the instructions, and there was my meal. This removed so many obstacles. So as you look at the tasks you have to implement to bring your Next Level into reality, ask yourself how you can remove obstacles and make the tasks easier for you to do.

Focus on the Smaller Task, Not the Results

I believe that where we trip ourselves up is that we are not patient, and/ or we get overwhelmed by the enormity of the goal. My advice is to break down the big goal into smaller tasks, tasks that you can complete easily. Let's say that the end result goal you have for yourself is to lose weight. Instead of saying, "I'm going to exercise for an hour every day, stop eating junk food, eat more healthily, and go to sleep at 10 p.m.," start with, "I'm going to walk around the block five mornings a week." Similarly, if you struggle with avoiding certain tasks at your job, you might focus on just one of those tasks and do it first thing in the morning when you get into the office.

When I first committed to raising money for the Leukemia & Lymphoma Society by running a marathon, I found that making the commitment was the easy step. It was the actual training that became challenging.

The first thing I did after I signed up to run the New York City Marathon was to take my car and drive exactly 26.2 miles, the length of a marathon. After that, I wanted to call my doctor to get a note to tell the Leukemia & Lymphoma Society that I couldn't do this. However, because I was already committed, backing out was not an option, so what I did was to break down my training into small steps.

For people who run marathons frequently, the endgame is to improve their time. In other words, they measure their success by the time it takes them to finish a marathon. In the level before that, runners focus on distance. This means that they might start off with a 5K, and once they finish that, consider it an accomplishment. The next step might be a half marathon, and once they finish that, that's their accomplishment. For me, I knew I had to break it down even smaller. My first accomplishment was just to wake up two hours earlier than usual, put on my jogging clothes, and go to my office, where my treadmill was. For the first two weeks, my goal wasn't distance and it wasn't time; it was just waking up early. Now, here's what I found: after two weeks, getting up two hours earlier was no longer a challenge. In other words, getting up early had become a new habit for me. Goal achieved!

My next goal was to just jog. I didn't have a goal for a specific distance or time. The goal was just getting on the treadmill and starting to move my body. After two more weeks, I had created two new habits: getting up two hours early and doing some sort of jogging. Boy, I was on fire now! My next goal was to start setting distance goals. And for a couple of weeks, if I jogged two to three miles, I was happy. I'm glad to say that after five months of working on this habit, in 2007 I finished the New York City Marathon. People sometimes ask me what my time was, and I joke, "Finished." The truth is, I'm lucky that I completed the race without my heart exploding out of my chest. Actually, the time is irrelevant (and so bad that I don't want to put it in print). The point is that I went from "no way can I do this" to actually accomplishing it.

Just focus on the task, and the results will come. Here's a little motivational expression that I learned when it comes to creating habits and tackling a project that seems too large to accomplish: "Inch by inch, life's a cinch; yard by yard, it's very hard."

Seek Out an Expert or Mentor

It's very possible, even likely, that there are other people who have mastered a skill in an area you need help in. Seek out those folks and get advice. Most successful people will tell you that they didn't do it alone. During their journey, they had other mentors they leaned on from time to time. For example, when I wanted to improve my humor and comedy delivery in my seminars, I turned to some real pros, such as comedy writer Frank Santopadre and stand-up comedienne Judy Carter. They were instrumental in punching up my delivery. Whenever I need business advice, I have a few experts to turn to. So, ask yourself the question, what areas do you need to be strong in if you are to achieve your Next Level? Now, you have to either get stronger in those areas or hire somebody who is already stronger in those areas to work for you. And I don't mean that you have to take on a whole staff of employees. There are a lot of virtual assistants who can work on certain projects and tasks that you delegate to them. And, again, there may be specific skill sets that you can't delegate, and that you need to get strong at yourself. For those areas, find a mentor who can give you some help.

Write a Letter to Yourself

Imagine that it's now 12 months later and you've accomplished all the items that you put on your Next Level paper. How will you feel? Remember what I wrote about *Star Trek* and how what we want in our lives already exists, but it just hasn't happened yet? Well, here is an exercise that will help train your brain to be more assertive in bringing your dreams into reality. What I want you to do is to write a letter to yourself congratulating yourself on the items that you've accomplished. Write this letter as if it's one year from now and you're standing in the future looking back at what you've achieved, giving yourself all sorts of accolades, and patting yourself on the back.

Let me share with you a segment from a letter that I wrote to myself when I did this exercise.

Dear Darryl,

Congratulations on getting your life back on track in accomplishing the things that are really important to yourself.

You've been a great father and your son has accomplished many great things. You couldn't ask for a better son. Congratulations on becoming an international speaker traveling around the world helping people design a life where they have less stress and more fun. I'm very proud of all that you've accomplished.

Now, if you want to have a lot of fun with this letter, here's what I encourage you to do. Take your letter, put it in an envelope, address it to yourself, put a stamp on it, and seal it. Then, take that sealed envelope, stick it in another envelope, and seal that one as well. Address the outer envelope to my address and mail it to me. I will hold onto your letter for 12 months from the time I receive it, at which time I will mail it back to you. I promise you I won't read it—I will keep it sealed, and when 12 months rolls around, I will mail it back to you. I cannot tell you the number of small miracles that have come about because of this simple step. Many times I have had students say to me, "Wow, Darryl . . . I just got the letter I wrote myself a year ago, and everything came true. Thank you so much!" To make sure you send it to my most recent address, please go to my website, www.DarrylSpeaks.com.

Smile Action Step

This chapter was mostly action steps you can implement to bring you closer to your Next Level. Right now, make a list of just two items that you are definitely going to implement over the next 30 days.

_____

_____

_____

_____

_____

_____

_____

_____

_____

_____

CHAPTER 7

WHY WE DO WHAT WE SHOULDN'T AND DON'T DO WHAT WE SHOULD

Accept the challenges, so that you may feel the exhilaration of victory.

—General George S. Patton

You must create positive habits if you are to make your dreams a reality. If you use the concepts that are discussed throughout this book, you will certainly create new habits and break old ones. In this chapter, I want to delve a little more deeply into the science behind habits.

It's important to understand that we are creatures of habit. Habits are things that we're programmed to do, not unlike the way a computer or a toy might be programmed. As we've discussed throughout this book, our past experiences become stored as neurological pathways and dictate how we think about love, relationships, our jobs, and other such things. And this "automatic thinking" determines the actions that we take moving forward. Each time we take the same action, we are carving a deeper pathway in our brain (and rewarding ourselves with comforting DOSEs of feel-good chemicals along the way). This is true both for familiar actions that are positive and those that are self-destructive.

Make or Break

Some habits are so automatic that we barely stop and think about all the little things that we accomplish before we even start our day. When you woke up this morning, you probably put on some clothes, brushed your teeth, combed your hair, made some coffee, and ate your breakfast. If we had to make a conscious decision about every action that we take every single day, we would wind up in a psych ward. So, if we can consciously create positive, goal-reinforcing habits that become automatic in the areas that are most important to us, we would be much more effective in our lives. But can everyone create these habits?

The reality is that habits are easier to make than they are to break. If you repeat a behavior often enough, those synaptic pathways are going to get reinforced. Everyone's brain is different, and habit formation also relies on aspects of experience and personality. There are many differing theories on how long it takes to create a habit. The previously accepted "magic number" was 21 days, but newer research seems to favor 66 days.[1] So, that means you need at least two months of consistent reinforcement to get this new behavior to the point where you don't have to exert a ton of effort to accomplish it, and it becomes automatic.

Breaking an old habit, however, is a bit more complicated, because once that neural pathway has been formed, it never really goes away.[2] It can weaken through lack of use, but it can easily be reactivated. "It is as though somehow, the brain retains a memory of the habit context, and this pattern can be triggered if the right habit cues come back," says researcher Ann Graybiel of MIT's McGovern Institute.[3] If you've ever tried to quit smoking, you already know this statement to be true. You can go a year without a cigarette, but if you give in one time, then *bam*, the habit comes right back. Of course, there are chemical components to that particular example, but the same holds true for other habits. The bottom line is that for most people, staying away from a bad habit is a lifetime effort.

The way to make this process easier is to form a new pattern within the same area as the one you are trying to break. You can replace the unwanted activity with the desired one. Let's say that your normal routine is to meet up with some of your friends after work a few times a week. You enjoy getting something to eat and having a drink or two. However, you are now coming to realize that this socializing is not affecting your waistline (or your bank account) in a positive way. So, what do you do? You could just stop going out with your friends altogether, *or* you could see if some of your friends would be up for taking a yoga class one or two nights a week. Substituting the yoga class for the restaurant visits will increase your chances of success substantially. You are getting the desired result of a healthier habit, but you didn't have to lose the reward of socializing with your friends. Building a rewarding parallel activity is the key to success when trying to break a bad habit.

There's a great fable that helps illustrate this point. As the story goes, there was a Cherokee chief who was teaching his grandson about a battle that goes on inside people. He said, "Always remember that there is a battle between 'two wolves' inside us all. The one wolf is Evil. It is anger, envy, jealousy, sorrow, regret, greed, arrogance, self-pity, guilt, resentment, inferiority, lies, false pride, superiority, and ego."

"The other wolf is Good. It is joy, peace, love, hope, serenity, humility, kindness, benevolence, empathy, generosity, truth, compassion, and faith." The grandson thought about it for a minute and then asked his grandfather, "Which one of the wolves will win?"

The old Cherokee simply replied, "The one you feed."

Although this story speaks specifically about personality traits, I think you could also easily apply it to more tangible actions as well. The Evil could be a bad habit that you are trying to conquer, such as, "spending too much money on your credit cards." In this case, the Good that you would want to nurture could be "putting away 10 percent of each paycheck." If you are consciously putting your energy and effort into something that you do want, the thing that you don't want will become weaker. With conscious nurturing, a desired trait can become second nature.

No matter how much you try, there's always going to be a tendency to listen to the evil wolf and fall back into unproductive or even destructive habits. That's why it's so important that you have a support structure that helps you stay focused on creating a new life that makes you smile.

Case Study: Brain Patterns

Ann Graybiel of MIT's McGovern Institute conducted an experiment to show how the brain changes when habits are formed.[4] In this experiment, rats learned that there was a chocolate reward at one end of a T-maze. While the rats were learning, scientists observed that their neurons were active throughout the maze run, as if everything might be important. As the rats learned which cues (audible tones) indicated the part of the maze that led to the chocolate, the neurons appeared to learn, too.

Once the rats had thoroughly learned the cues, the neurons that were involved in the task fired intensely at the parts of the task they were most involved in—the beginning and the end. But those neurons became quiet as the rats ran through the recognizable part of the maze, as if they were so familiar with the maze that it wasn't exciting for them anymore. Then the researchers removed the reward, making the cues meaningless. This change in training made everything in the maze relevant again, and the neurons once more were active throughout the run. The rats eventually stopped running (gave up the habit), and the new habit pattern of the brain cells disappeared. But as soon as the researchers returned the reward, the learned neural pattern, with the same beginning and ending spikes, appeared again.

Analysts theorized that this experiment shows how a learned pattern remains in the brain even after the behavior is extinguished, further demonstrating how easy it is to fall back into familiar habits.

You've probably heard of a concept called *muscle memory*. When a movement is repeated over time, a long-term muscle memory is created for that task, eventually allowing it to be performed without conscious effort. Examples of muscle memory are found in many everyday activities that become automatic and improve with practice, such as riding a bicycle, typing on a keyboard, playing an instrument, and playing video games. Creating a habit works in the same way, except that it is not a muscle that is being trained, but a neural pathway that is being created and reinforced.

Case Study: Willpower and Bad Habits

When you are replacing a bad habit with a good one, it's important that you pick one habit at a time, and the reason is that we have a limited amount of willpower. When we focus on making a major change, such as creating a new habit that is difficult for us to do, we have to put a lot of energy into creating that one habit. Therefore, it's really hard for us to concentrate and focus on other important tasks that require a tremendous amount of additional willpower and energy.

A renowned researcher by the name of Roy Baumeister studied this very concept.[5] In one of his studies, he invited college students into a lab and instructed them not to eat anything for at least three hours prior to their arrival. He then separated the students into three groups. Group 1 was put in a room with two plates of food. One plate held chocolate chip cookies, and the other one was a plate of radishes. They were instructed that they were not to eat the chocolate chip cookies, but they were free to eat as many radishes as they wanted. Group 2 was put in a room with the same two plates, but they were told that they could eat off of either plate. Group 3 was put into a room with no food at all. Then all three groups were asked to solve a geometric puzzle. The truth was that the puzzle was unsolvable, but the students were not told this.

Here was the result of the study: no one solved the puzzle, of course, but those in Group 1 threw up their hands and quit long before those in Groups 2 and 3. Why? Because those in Group 1 had to use every ounce of their willpower to avoid eating the chocolate chip cookies and therefore didn't have the mental energy left to focus on the complex puzzle. This tells us that we have a limited amount of willpower. If we put too much stress on ourselves by trying to break a bad habit and create a positive habit, all the while taking on a mentally challenging task, we are probably going to quit much earlier than if we tackle one thing at a time.

Smile Action Steps

✳ Looking at your *bad* habits, what are one or two habits that you would like to do away with?

_____

_____

_____

_____

_____

_____

_____

✳ What are one or two *good* habits that you would like to create?

_____

_____

_____

_____

_____

_____

_____

✳ Now, choose one good habit to create *or* one bad habit to break that you would like to work for the next 66 days.

_____

_____

_____

_____

_____

_____

_____

* If you choose to break a bad habit, remember that you must, at the same time, replace that habit with a positive action in order to retrain the synaptic pathways in your brain. If you do not do this, you are probably going to fail at breaking that habit. So what positive activity can you do to replace the bad habit? What support structure can you put in place to help you stay focused and committed to getting rid of the bad habit with this new activity?

_____

_____

_____

_____

_____

_____

_____

THE KEY INGREDIENT TO TAKING CONTROL OF YOUR LIFE

Better keep yourself clean and bright; you are the window through which you must see the world.

—George Bernard Shaw

After all my years of coaching people how to take control of their lives, I have learned that one of the most important ingredients in accomplishing this control is to have a high level of integrity. Now, when discussing the concept of *integrity*, many people initially think of major issues—for example, cheating, lying, or stealing. But I would suggest that these issues are just a portion of what we have to take a look at when it comes to designing a life worth smiling about.

I like to break the idea of integrity into two simple categories: the "big things" and the "small things." For our purposes in this book, we can skip the big things—I don't think I need to tell you that integrity and crime don't go hand in hand. (If you are thinking about committing a crime, please seek professional help immediately.)

So let's talk about the second category, the small things. Let me share with you one of my favorite quotes on integrity, by the famous former mayor of New York City, Ed Koch:

Our personal integrity is tested all the time. An honest person believes he demonstrates it by never stealing or otherwise engaging in unethical conduct. He's generally on solid ground when the stakes are high. But it is the small things that provide the real test.

My good friend and real estate mentor, and for a while someone whom I would say was a second father to me, Mac Levitt, and I were discussing how important the small things are. Mac shared an analogy with me that I must warn you is a little graphic—but it clearly illustrates how the little things in our lives can have a big impact when it comes to our integrity. Mac said to me, "Imagine that I have a big bowl of punch. I mean, this thing is huge. We're talking four feet in diameter. And if I take a shot glass filled with urine and pour it into one side of the bowl, would you drink from the other side?" Of course, being a silly young man, my response was, "Well, it depends on how thirsty I am." But of course the real answer, which I think would be true for any of us, is that I wouldn't drink the punch at all.

That bowl of punch represents everything that makes up a human being: her character, her relationships, her goals, and her aspirations. The urine represents every time we make a promise that we don't keep, every time we say that we'll be somewhere at a certain time and show up late, or every time that we tell a little white lie that won't hurt anyone. Yes, it may be small, but it does affect the character of a person's life.

A Life of Integrity

Let's look at the definition of integrity. It might surprise you to discover that it means much more than keeping promises or not stealing.

According to merriam-webster.com, the definition of integrity is:

> 1: *firm adherence to a code of especially moral or artistic*
>   *values:* INCORRUPTIBILITY
> 2: *an unimpaired condition:* SOUNDNESS
> 3: *the quality or state of being complete or undivided:*
>   COMPLETENESS

Living a life of integrity is not a goal that you ultimately achieve. Instead, it's something that you are constantly looking to improve upon and a place to live from. It's a concept similar to mastering karate. I've heard sensei teach that when you get to the level of black belt, the end result is not the belt, but a way of life. You're always working on your art and your craft of mastery. Living a life committed to integrity is very much the same thing.

We are going to make mistakes. We are going to break promises and not show up when we say we're going to show up. This is part of being human. The difference between the person who lives a life that is committed to integrity and the one who doesn't is that the one who *doesn't* always has an excuse ready to use. He excuses away something (or many things) every single day! He says things like, "I got stuck in traffic," "So-and-so didn't do what she was supposed to, so I couldn't do what I was supposed to," or, "I missed our 2 p.m. conference call because my previous meeting started an hour late." In other words, he tries to absolve himself for the results that he himself produced. On the contrary, someone who's committed to integrity takes full responsibility for his or her actions.

One of the greatest motivational speakers, in my opinion, was Zig Ziglar. And one of my favorite quotes that Zig often used was, "When you point your finger at the problem, there's three fingers pointing back at you." People who make excuses think that they are letting themselves off the hook by avoiding blame for something, but what they are really doing is robbing themselves of the power that comes from being in control of their own life. Whenever you blame circumstances when something goes wrong, you put yourself at the mercy of external forces that you're saying you can't do anything about. When you live from a commitment to integrity, however, you start to have some power and control over how your life looks. This helps you avoid the syndrome of coming across as a victim.

"But, Darryl," I can hear you thinking, "there are times when I literally *can't* attend a meeting because something else runs late. That's not an excuse, that's reality!" Good point. But keep in mind that what we are discussing here is how to create a life that's worth smiling about—how to create your own reality that motivates and empowers you. While it's true that you may miss a meeting, the reason for this is that you made a *choice* to miss it when the other meeting ran late. Take responsibility for that choice! Check this out. As I said earlier, a typical person might say, "I missed our 2 p.m. conference call because my previous meeting started an hour late." Here's what a person living with high integrity would say (and, by the way, you would alert the people in the later meeting *in advance*, not after the fact): "I am involved in a meeting right now that's running late. I'm going to stay in this meeting and would like to reschedule," or, "and I'd like to touch base with you later to get the summary of what was discussed." Can you see the difference? In one case, you are blaming external forces. In the other, you are taking responsibility for what is happening around you and powerfully and proactively choosing how to respond. It's vitally important that you learn to be the cause in your life rather than simply display the effects.

Now, what does this have to do with living a life worth smiling about? I believe that a lot of the reason for stress in our lives is that we spend a lot of energy and time trying to clean up our mistakes, when what we should really be doing is taking full responsibility for the outcomes we produce. All of this cleanup effort is exhausting and unproductive.

The story of Wally Amos, the famous King of Cookies, will help illustrate what I mean. As the story goes, Wally learned to bake cookies at a young age. His first job out of college was as a talent agent, and he used his baking skills to attract clients by making them chocolate chip cookies. His cookies were so good that he ended up opening a successful storefront in Los Angeles, and eventually selling them to stores nationwide. He brought in some investors when he started having financial issues, and he was eventually voted out of his own company.

So Wally thought to himself, "No problem. I'll just start another company." He attempted to create another cookie company, but his previous business then sued him, stating that he was not allowed to use his name on any food product. So let's recap. Not only had he been fired from the company that he created, but he had lost the rights to use his name on any food product. As I watched this story unfold in a television interview, the interviewer made this statement to Wally: "You must've been devastated. If it were me, I don't think I could go on." Wally responded, saying something I'll never forget: "I'm totally fine with what occurred because I know that I created these problems in my life, and therefore I also know that I have it in me to produce solutions to solve those problems."

Wally took full responsibility for the results he produced in his life, both the good and the bad. Such an attitude shows that you have integrity and are responsible for the promises you make—you do not play the role of the victim. When you internalize this sentiment, not just in your head but in your heart, then you will have much more power in your life. And when you speak the words, "Here's how my life is going to look in the future," the universe will listen to you because the universe knows that you are a person who keeps her word. You are a person who is committed to living a life of integrity.

In his book *The Seven Habits of Highly Effective People*,[1] author Stephen R. Covey gives this insight into integrity:

> *Honesty is telling the truth—in other words, conforming our words to reality.* Integrity is conforming reality to our words—*in other words, keeping promises and fulfilling expectations.*

Here are three suggestions to help you get started with improving your integrity. If you work on these, you're going to see mini-miracles in your life.

1. *Stop doing what you don't want anybody to know about.* How does that saying go: Everybody's got dirty little secrets? Well, I know there was a song and a movie with that title, so I guess there might be some truth in it. But consider this. There are two things you can't hide from: yourself and the universe. (The definition of the *universe* will vary from person to person. If you're spiritual, it could be a deity or some form of higher consciousness; if you're more secular, it refers to anything external that might support you in getting to your Next Level.) If you tell the universe that you're doing one thing, but behind closed doors you're doing another, then you are not living by your word. So when you set goals or commit yourself to achieving a Next Level, the universe will not support you because the universe "sees" you as someone who doesn't keep his word. I know you probably hate me right now, but hey, I didn't write this rule, the universe did.

2. *Clean up past relationships.* Remember our dictionary definition for integrity earlier in this chapter? One meaning is "the quality or state of being complete or undivided: COMPLETENESS." When you have something unsaid that sits in the corner of your mind, this is an incomplete item. If you avoid a person or a task, that item, by definition, is incomplete. So, you might have somebody in your life whom you have stopped talking to because you had an argument or some kind of disagreement. Usually, when this happens, we hold onto the anger, judgments, and negative thoughts about that person. Why else would we still not be talking to him? These emotions, thoughts, and feelings cre-

ate more baggage that weighs us down and steals our joy. It's time for you to consider mending some fences. Now, I'm not saying that you should call every Tom, Dick, and Jane to kiss and make up. I do believe that there are some toxic relationships in the world, and you may be better off not being around those people. You have to ask yourself whether the person whom you stopped talking to was the problem, or whether you were the negative influence on the relationship at the time. Although it may be difficult to answer, only you know the truth about that question. If you were being toxic, it might be a good idea for you to reach out to that person and attempt to get rid of the baggage, let go of the judgments, and try to rebuild your relationship with her. Why? Not for her benefit, but for yours. Here's a little side note: usually the things that are hardest for us to do are where the biggest growth occurs. *It takes a really powerful person to stop being upset or angry with somebody, and be committed to the possibility of having a relationship with that person again.* This would also be a tremendous weight lifted off your shoulders. Cleaning up a relationship will free you to be more productive and happier.

3. *Get your home in order.* Make a list of all the things in your house that are draining your energy and start to do something about them. For example, you might have a drawer in your house that has all these lonely keys in it, and you don't know which locks they belong to. Somehow, you think that the locks and keys are going to miraculously hook up with each other all by themselves. What do you say to yourself every time you pass that drawer? I bet you say something like this: "I've got to clean out that drawer someday." Well, guess what? Every time you walk past that drawer with that thought, the drawer is sucking energy out of you. Not much, just a little bit, but it's still an integrity issue. It's

something that you've left incomplete and have avoided. Or you have that pile of things that needs to be dealt with in the home. Or there's that doorknob that you keep meaning to fix. Or there are those clothes: either you're hoping that they will come back into style or you're hoping that you'll lose 20 pounds in your sleep so that they will fit the next morning. All these things are just little integrity issues. They drain your energy. So make that list and schedule half a day each week to get to those items. Now, as you work on that, new things may show up that need to be added to that list. As a matter of fact, this list may never be completed, but at least you're living from integrity by doing something about it rather than internally complaining about it or avoiding it entirely. Start to make a list of a few things now:

1. _____

2. _____

3. _____

4. _____

5. _____

The Power of Your Words

When it comes to integrity, the language that we use is crucial. Our words matter. When we make a commitment and tell someone that we're going to do something, we need to keep our word. When we make a promise to ourselves, we need to follow through. When we set our Next Level goals, we need to do what it takes to continuously move toward them. It all starts with our speaking. With our words, we are creating a reality for ourselves and for those we communicate with.

THE KEY INGREDIENT TO TAKING CONTROL OF YOUR LIFE

I read an article in *Sports Illustrated* in which the reporter interviewed three umpires. The first umpire had just started his career as an umpire. The second umpire had been in the job for about 10 years, and the third one had been in the business for about 20 years. The reporter asked all three of them, "How do you know when to call a ball or a strike?" The first umpire said, "I call it how I see it"; the second umpire said, "I call it how it is"; and the third umpire said, "It isn't anything yet until I call it."

Now that's real power! Think about that statement: until that umpire says what it is, it really isn't anything. In other words, it doesn't exist until the umpire makes the call. (Consider this for a moment. Have you ever watched a baseball game where the umpire takes a long time to call the pitch? If so, you know this statement is true. The pitch is neither a ball nor a strike until the umpire says so.) So, there is a tremendous amount of power in what you say. People have been inspired by words, companies have been created, and even nations have been invented.

For the past several years, it's been a tradition in our family to spend the Fourth of July in Washington, DC. On one of our annual trips, I took my family to see Ford's Theatre, where President Lincoln was shot. Hanging in the museum, there is a copy of President Lincoln's Gettysburg Address. I thought it was important for my son to understand how powerful words can be and how important his speaking is. So, after we read it, I said to him,

"What amazes me is not that the speech inspired a nation, or that after a couple of hundred years we're still talking about it. It doesn't surprise me that this speech has been etched in granite on a monument in honor of an incredible human being. What does amaze me is the fact that this speech consists of only 272 words. To me, that's the brilliant thing. Because the right words were used in the right order at the right time, it was able to inspire a nation." I wanted my son to know that as he gets older and masters the English language, maybe he too can inspire people with just his speaking.

Smile Action Steps

1. *Get more rigorous with your own integrity.* You will notice that I did not say that you should be perfect in all areas of your life. Of course not. It's very rare to find a person who has 100 percent perfect integrity, but what you can do is kick your integrity up a notch. Be a little more "squeaky clean." Do your best to improve the quality of your life by being more complete and whole with the people and items (like your drawer of keys) around you. If you start to really focus on living a life of integrity, and you truly pay more attention to keeping your promises (especially the small ones) and being truthful in all areas of your life, including with yourself, you will notice something miraculous. The universe will start to align with you and give you what you want because you say so. It's almost as if you get rewarded from the "Universal Bank of Karma."

2. *Everything you say is a promise.* Get serious and strict with yourself. For example, if you promise to be somewhere at a certain time, be there. If you wind up showing up late, don't excuse it away. Take responsibility, apologize, and make a commitment to that person that you will never break your promise again when it comes to showing up when you say you're going to show up.

3. *Do an integrity checkup.* Integrity is one of the most important ingredients in having power in your speaking. Go through the following six questions and see if you can make some progress on cleaning up some things in your life that may need cleaning up.

   a. *Where in my life am I not living consistently with who I say I am? (Where is my heartache, my pain, my anger, or my blame?)*

   _____

   _____

   _____

_____

_____

b. *Where do I continue to break promises, and what is the pay-off I get from that? (I say that I will do X, and never do it.)*

_____

_____

_____

_____

_____

c. *What parts of my life am I in denial about?*

_____

_____

_____

_____

_____

d. *How much of my thinking, feeling energy is directed toward my past . . . toward the failed relationships, betrayals, emotional/physical issues, and other violations to myself? (When we have part of our energy in the past, we are not whole in the present, and therefore we are out of integrity.)*

_____

_____

_____

_____

_____

e. *Are there times that I remain silent about things that I know without question are wrong?*

_____

_____

_____

_____

_____

f. *Take a moment and write down three areas where you have been out of integrity—it could be that you lied to someone, have been out of communication, or even didn't give your full effort to something that you knew you should. While you're at it, write down due dates for "by when" you'll set these instances right.*

_____

_____

_____

_____

_____

CHAPTER 9

LETTING GO OF YOUR PAST AND MOVING FORWARD

Forgiveness is a most powerful weapon because it frees you from the bondage that comes with holding onto anger. When you hold onto anger, it's actually anger that's holding onto you.

—Author Unknown

One of the things we absolutely need to do if we are to have a life worth smiling about is to forgive more. We need to forgive ourselves and even forgive others who have wronged us. When we hang onto resentment and negative feelings, we create baggage in our life that weighs us down. It's just like when you check in at the airport; if you have extra baggage, it costs you. Well, in life, when you have extra baggage, it also costs you—obviously not in a monetary sense, but I'd say that these costs are way more important. As discussed in the previous chapter, hanging onto past hurt, anger, and regrets will cost you your energy and peace of mind.

When we don't forgive someone, whether it's ourselves or others, we are hanging onto something that happened in the past, something that no longer exists. Every time we think of that painful memory, focus on it, complain about it, share it with others, or dwell on it, we are literally bringing our past into our present, which prevents us from creating a future that really makes us smile.

Here's an acronym that may help you to forgive yourself and others more quickly: PAST.

Predictable. If we focus on the past, we are living from the past. And if we live from the past, we are creating a future that isn't based on possibility. Do you know some people who, no matter what job they have (or what boss they have), seem to keep complaining about the same thing? That's an example of someone who's living from the past (when they keep complaining about it) and creating a *predictable* future.

Anchor. Living from the past anchors us and weighs us down. It keeps us from moving forward in our life.

Sacrifice. When you do not forgive yourself or others, you sacrifice joy, happiness, and being complete in your life. Instead, you experience fear, sadness, resentment, and even hatred.

Tired. When you're living from your past, complaining about your past, thinking about your past, or wishing that your past was different, that just tires you out (just like when you carry too much baggage through the airport terminals)!

Drop Your Baggage and Forgive

Part of letting go and moving forward is to forgive yourself! Upsets, mistakes, bad decisions, fights with others—they all occurred in the past. You can't change or fix them. So what do you do with them? Leave them alone! Let them be! A mistake from your past is similar to a wound on your body that has a scab on it. I know this is not a pleasant visual, but hang in there with me. Every time you pick the scab, you reopen the wound. You need to leave it alone and give it time to heal.

When you make a mistake, every time you feel guilty or beat yourself up about it, the destructiveness of that initial action is being played out yet again. Instead, redeem yourself by doing something positive and constructive in your life. When you live from your past, it's like driving a car while staring at your rearview mirror. One of two things will happen: you will crash, or you will end up in an entirely different place from where you wanted to be.

One of the best parts of my job is that I get to travel all over the world. Two of my favorite places to visit are Australia and New Zealand. Not only are the people wonderful, but the scenery is breathtaking. On my first trip to New Zealand, I decided to take my family hot-air ballooning. Once we were up in the atmosphere, I thought of a question to ask the balloonist. (In retrospect, I probably should've asked him this while we were still on the ground.) I asked him, "How do you steer this thing?" After he stopped laughing, he explained to me that there are air currents, just like there are currents in the ocean. Some go left, some go right, some go forward, and some go back. He explained to me that you have to find the current that's going in the direction that you want to go and ride that current.

That got me to thinking that hot-air ballooning is like our lives. If your balloon of life is not going in the direction that you want it to go, you can complain to and yell at the wind, talk to your friends about the wind, or even set up a committee meeting in the basket to talk about what the wind is doing. But the wind doesn't care what you think, how loudly you yell at it, or how many conversations you have with your friends about it. *It cares only about what you do.* What you have to do is drop your baggage so that you can rise to a new level and ride the current that's going to bring you where you want to go. In order to get to the Next Level in your life, part of the process is letting go of your baggage, whether it's with yourself or other people. You've got to forgive. Forgiveness is the release mechanism that drops the baggage.

For me, one of the bags that I had to let go of was the death of my father. When he passed away, I was 14 years old. I was obviously upset about losing my father, but most of my upsets were normal things that a son who was fairly close to his father would feel. There was this one piece of baggage, however, that I couldn't shake, one major thing that caused a tremendous amount of guilt that was holding me down through my late teens. That regret was that I had never told my father that I loved him. As a 14-year-old, I rationally knew that he must have known what my feelings were. I was certain that he loved me, after all, and he couldn't have loved me as much as he did if he didn't know that I loved him, right? But, as you know, when you really regret something, the emotional side rather than the rational side takes charge. As I look back, I see how this major baggage in my life held me back in so many ways. As a teenager, I was a bit of an angry fellow; I was arrogant, thinking that I could take care of myself and would never have to open myself up to loving again.

It was only at age 19 that I gained a sort of "completeness" and I truly knew (in my head and in my heart) that my father knew that I loved him—whether I had told him so or not. I also made a commitment that I would never feel that regret again. I learned the lesson that when people are important to me, I make sure that I let them know. I make sure that I tell them that I love them. I forgave myself, and I grew as a person from the experience.

Here are four other ways to help yourself find closure and drop your excess baggage with regard to a loved one who may no longer be with you:

1. Talk to someone. Confide in a friend, or someone you feel can help you come to terms with this issue.
2. If you believe in a higher power, pray to that higher power on a regular basis and have a conversation with your loved one in those prayers.
3. Write a letter to your loved one expressing everything you feel about her, with the intention of having closure.
4. Recognize that the feelings of regret or frustration that you might have are once again your chemical brain at work. Sometimes just knowing that your feelings are automatic and are chemically created by your past experiences means that they can begin to have less control over you.

Forgiving Others

The second area of forgiving that we need to be skilled in is forgiving others. When you're not complete with yourself *or* with others, it drains you. For instance, have you ever been driving on the road when somebody cuts you off and you yell at him, then you go on being upset about this incident for the next couple of hours? You might share this experience with friends at the office; you might call your significant other to complain about this horrible driver. So, now you hold on to this anger for hours, and all you accomplish is letting the anger rob you of your joy.

Let me tell you about a crazy incident that happened to me at the airport. I was in the parking lot, and I drove down one aisle to the next. I saw somebody pull out of this great spot, so I drove into the space. After I turned the car engine off, and I was sitting in the driver's seat getting ready to open my door, somebody was suddenly standing alongside my car. He yelled at me, "You're in my parking spot!" I said, "Excuse me?" through the closed glass. (In New York, when a stranger comes up to your door and starts tapping on the glass, it's a good idea to keep your door locked.) He again yelled, "You're in my parking spot!" Of course, I was very confused, since there are no assigned parking spots at the airport, and I even said to the gentleman, "Well, if I'm in your spot, how come my car is here and not yours? If it were your spot, your car would be here." To which he responded that he had been parked in a handicapped spot waiting for a good spot close to the entrance. I mean, I couldn't make this up if I wanted to.

At this point I could've had a battle of wits with this gentleman, and I certainly would've won the conversation. But this guy was so upset that I had to ask myself the question, "Am I committed to winning an argument with this guy, or am I committed to having more joy in my life?" If I continued this argument with him, I would've continued to get more upset or stressed (not to mention the fact that, after I got on the plane, I'd be wondering the whole time whether my car would still be there when I got back from my trip). So, here's what I said to the gentleman: "Well, obviously this parking spot is very important in your life, and for that reason, I'll be happy to give it to you." Once I pulled out of the spot, I found another spot three cars closer to the entrance than the original spot. This made me think that this was something of a metaphor—that sometimes we are fighting for a parking spot in life, and that parking spot is our opinions about what we think people should be doing and how they should be acting or treating us. As part of mastering the art of forgiveness, you first have to master letting go of your opinions. Sometimes when we fight for our parking spot, we might win, which actually makes us lose. The winner is the one who can let go of the argument and move on with her life without ever looking back.

Learn to forgive yourself and others, and learn to do it quickly. The longer you hang onto baggage and unresolved situations, the more precious time you're wasting.

Live in the Present

As human beings, we have a tendency to worry about what's going to happen tomorrow and to be upset about what happened yesterday, both at the same time. When we do this, we're truly not appreciating where we are right at this moment. It reminds me of the saying, "If you have one eye on yesterday and one eye on tomorrow, you're going to be cockeyed today." However, I'm going to guess that since you're reading this book, there's a good chance that you are "being present" right this second. You'll notice that it's hard to read this book and think about what you're going to do tomorrow or worry about what you did yesterday. As a matter of fact, if there was any point when you were reading this book when you drifted off thinking about yesterday or tomorrow, that probably stopped you from reading or forced you to go back and reread because you weren't fully present at the moment. This is a perfect example of how worrying about what tomorrow is going to bring or about what happened yesterday prevents you from enjoying your life today.

Here's an example of us not being present. Have you ever been in a conversation or a meeting at work when, as someone is talking, you are thinking about what you are going to say when he or she finishes? It can be difficult to pay attention to a conversation with someone else when we get stuck listening to that little voice inside our head. As someone else is talking, we're actually thinking about and listening to what we're going to say next. When you're in a conversation and you're focused on that voice inside your head, you're not truly being present. You're not getting the point of the other person's communication because you're distracted and focused on yourself. Not only can this self-centeredness and distraction negatively affect your performance at work, but it will also affect the way you interact with others in your personal life.

A couple of years ago, I was holding a seminar at the University of Maryland. The university has an interesting setup because it has a hotel that's attached to the campus meeting rooms. There's a link from the hotel lobby to the meeting rooms, and you have to walk down this very long hallway to get to the other side. It almost feels as if the university created the hallway as a sort of tunnel to get you from the hotel to the meeting room space. It was the night before the event, and, as always, I like to check my meeting room to get a feel for the space, and also to bring over some of my equipment, handouts, and the like. I had to make a couple of trips along this corridor. After going down the hallway a second time, I noticed that there was this beautiful artwork on display. I caught myself, stopped hustling and bustling, and took the time to enjoy the artwork. I spent a good 30 minutes going from piece to piece to appreciate each artist's work. I thought to myself, "What if I had continued just running down the hallway?" I certainly would've missed out on this opportunity to appreciate my surroundings. How many other times have I done this in my life when I've been rushing to get somewhere and missed out on the artwork of my life that was right there in front of me? There is so much art in our lives: our relationships, our accomplishments, even strangers on the street. All of these are things for us to appreciate, and we should take the time to go through life just a little bit more slowly, so that we can be present in the moment.

Here's another example. Not too long ago, I went to Disney World with my family. Like a lot of amusement parks today, it has a phone app that gives you a map of the park showing the attractions and waiting times. It even lets you make reservations at the restaurants. To make sure that I optimized our time, I was trying to map out the best approach: decide which rides we should go on next based on the waiting time, then coordinate this with our lunch and dinner. I spent more time staring at my phone and playing with the app than I did appreciating being *in* the park!

Sometimes, we can be that way with our goals when we focus on trying to get somewhere perfectly, and we plan and we strategize over and over again. Meanwhile, we're not appreciating where we are in the moment. Make a conscious effort to take a deep breath and appreciate your surroundings. Don't take your present life for granted while you're planning your Next Level.

Smile Action Steps

* Think of someone you can call to reestablish communication. (In Chapter 14 I discuss how to have this conversation.) Remember, it may not be that you need to forgive him or her for some sort of transgression. It might be that you yourself have to let go of some guilt. But please keep in mind, either way, you definitely don't want to come across as though you are doing the person a favor by "letting him or her off the hook."

Not everyone is seeking your forgiveness, and you are not doing this as a favor. You are doing it to be complete and because you honestly mean it.

_____

_____

_____

_____

_____

_____

* Think of one regret or mistake you've made that you keep beating yourself up about. Write it here, and as you do, commit to forgiving yourself and letting it go once and for all!

_____

_____

_____

_____

_____

_____

* Did you have a relationship with someone close to you who has passed away, and do you have some baggage about that relationship? Is there something you wish you had said to him before he passed? If so, take the time to write a letter to him as if he were still alive, saying what you need to say in order to get complete. After you write the letter, either save it or throw it away. This process is about your getting complete, letting go, and moving forward.

_____

_____

_____

_____

_____

_____

* There may be some areas in your life (especially those areas that have become mundane) where you have a tendency to not be present. What are those times when you feel unfocused or connected to what's happening? When do you have a tendency not to be present? List those times now and make a commitment to being more present in the future.

_____

_____

_____

_____

_____

_____

CHAPTER 10

BE KIND TO YOURSELF— YOU DESERVE IT

There is more to life than increasing its speed.

—Mahatma Gandhi

Do you ever compare yourself to others? Do you sometimes wish you had someone else's life because on the surface, his or her life looks better than yours? Well, that type of thinking actually robs you of joy and causes you to lose appreciation for what you have in your life. Let me give you some thoughts to help you stop that stinkin' thinkin'.

Run Your Own Race

First, you need to understand this important fact: most people only show you what they want to show you about themselves. You may think that someone has a great house, car, marriage, children, and job, but I promise you, you're seeing only what that person wants you to see. In my many years of coaching people, I can tell you with all certainty that you would be surprised if you knew what was going on behind the scenes of the lives of those folks you admire. And it's very possible that if you knew about the parts of their lives that you don't see, you wouldn't want to be in their shoes!

Second, there are people who have more challenges and life issues than you do, and they look at *your* life with envy. In fact, they wish they had your life.

Here's the bottom line: the only person you should compare yourself to is yourself. Let me ask you a question: Are you a better person now than you were five years ago? Ten years ago? Were you dealing with some major life issues, and at the time you didn't think you would get through them? I bet that if you look at how far you have come in your life, you would be really proud of yourself. Focus on how far you have come from where you *used* to be, not how far you are from where you *want* to be.

When I was training to run the New York City Marathon, I happened to be in Los Angeles, California, to do a seminar. I was staying at a swanky hotel, and it had an incredible gym on a very high floor. It had the best equipment, and from ceiling to floor were these glass windows where you could look out over Los Angeles. Every treadmill had its own LCD TV hanging in front of it. So, I was there on the treadmill doing my thing, and in walked a guy who could have been Brad Pitt's body double. He was gorgeous, thin, and perfect in his tank top, and he got onto the machine right next to me and started running. I don't even know if I should use the word *running*—he was barely touching the machine; it was as if he was *floating.* Now, I was running right next to him. If you looked over at me, you would think I was about to have a heart attack. So when I looked at him, I thought to myself that I must be crazy to think that I could run a marathon. This guy next to me, *he* could run a marathon. He's got a marathon body. I'm lucky if I can live through the training, let alone the actual race.

Then I corrected my thinking. I thought to myself, "Wait a second. I should be proud of the fact that I'm even on this treadmill." If you had asked me six months earlier if I'd be running five to seven miles every single day, I would've thought you were nuts. What I was doing was a huge accomplishment! My final thought to myself was: "Darryl, run your race, not his!"—the point being, don't get trapped in comparing your life to somebody else's. You may compare yourself to others and think they are better off than you are, but believe me, they have blemishes too. And, in any case, it doesn't matter, because the bottom line is that you need to live your own life.

Here's a Japanese fable that I would like to share with you to help illustrate this point. A samurai came upon a monk who was praying. When the monk had finished his prayers, the samurai asked, "Why do I feel so inferior? I have faced death many times, have defended those who are weak. Nevertheless, upon seeing you meditating, I felt that my life had absolutely no importance whatsoever."

"Wait," the monk said. "Once I have attended to all those who come to see me today, I shall answer you."

The samurai spent the whole day sitting in the temple gardens, watching the people go in and out in search of advice. He saw how the monk received them all with the same patience and the same smile on his face. At nightfall, when everyone had gone, the samurai demanded: "Now can you teach me?"

The master invited him in and led him to his room. The full moon shone in the sky, and the atmosphere was one of profound tranquility.

"Do you see the moon, how beautiful it is? It will cross the entire firmament, and tomorrow the sun will shine once again," the monk remarked.

"But sunlight is much brighter, and can show the details of the landscape around us: trees, mountains, and clouds," said the samurai.

"I have contemplated the two for years, and I have never heard the moon say: 'Why do I not shine like the sun? Is it because I am inferior?'" said the monk.

"Of course not," answered the samurai. "The moon and the sun are different things; each has its own beauty. You cannot compare the two."

"So you know the answer," said the monk. "We are two different people, each fighting in his own way for that which he believes, and making it possible to make the world a better place; the rest are mere appearances."

Be Healthy

Honestly, I almost didn't include this topic in the book because this is *not* my strength. I generally have only two food groups: pasta and pastries!

But seriously, being healthy is important for so many reasons: you feel better, you have more energy, it puts less stress on your body, and therefore you smile more. But let me tell you the biggest benefit of getting healthier: it takes a tremendous commitment and focus in order to have a breakthrough in your physical well-being. And, for some of you, this could absolutely transform your life. If you are one of those people who is already healthy or in shape, I applaud you for your commitment and willpower. It is not an easy thing.

I'm not saying that you should become healthy just to be healthy. I don't think you should do anything that you don't want to do. But I will tell you this: when you accomplish the thing that is the hardest for you to accomplish, that's when the biggest breakthroughs occur. (I devote an entire chapter of this book [Chapter 13] to what I call "breakdowns" and "breakthroughs." For the purpose of this discussion, consider a breakthrough to be an event in which you surpass your previous limitations—self-imposed or otherwise—and achieve a life-changing result.) Why? Because if you can overcome the biggest challenge you're having in your life right now, when you walk away from that accomplishment, you'll feel as if you can accomplish anything. The moment you are ready to seriously commit to having a breakthrough in your health, that's when the rest of your life is really going to soar.

There is another benefit to improving your health: it's hard to be confident about other areas in your life when you feel physically out of shape. (Can I get an "amen" from those of you who are already healthy?) For those of you who are struggling with your health and your weight, let me give you a couple of suggestions that might help.

* *Your willpower bank account.* Let's pretend that you have a bank account and that each day you start off with $100. Now, as you spend that money throughout the day, obviously your bank account gets depleted. That's what willpower is. It's crucial that you don't try to take on too many major things in your life at the same time. You simply can't follow through on every commitment you make, particularly in an area as vital as your health, if you say, "I'm going to lose 20 pounds, so what I'm going to start doing is going to the gym every day for two hours, and I'm going to eat nothing but steamed vegetables. I'm going to become a vegetarian, I'm going to cut out all the carbs in my life, and while I'm at it, I'm going to go back to college to earn a degree."

  In this example, if you have $100 of willpower, you just spent $250. We can't accomplish many of the goals we set because we take on more than we can emotionally handle. So, if you have a major project that you need to accomplish (and losing weight is a big undertaking), you need to choose just one of those items to tackle at a time, because unless you are super-human, chances are that you will not succeed in doing all of them at the same time.

* *Create one good health habit.* We also said earlier in the book that it's important to focus on creating new habits. Remember that it is easier for our brain to focus on what we *want*, so make sure that you set your goals appropriately. If you focus on cutting out negative habits, you will automatically be focused only on those habits, and ending them will be harder to accomplish. There are, however, some really simple steps that will get you on the right path. As basic as they sound, they will absolutely have an impact on your well-being. Here are a few suggestions:

  * Drink more water.
  * Get enough sleep.
  * Add some type of physical activity to your day.
  * Eat smaller meals.

As I said, these are *basic*, but if you embrace one small change and master it, you will feel better, and then you'll be ready to take things a step further. Once you have developed those two habits, and you're not using too much willpower to maintain them, then you can use your willpower for the next habit that you want to create. If you tried to do all these things at the same time, you would probably go nuts. Remember what I said way back in Chapter 6: "Inch by inch, life's a cinch; yard by yard, it's very hard."

Have Faith That You'll Get There

When it comes to faith, I'm not talking solely about religion.

Although having religious faith can be incredibly empowering and helpful, in this section I want to talk to you more about having faith in the Next Level that you're committed to accomplishing. This type of faith is the activator that helps you attract all the resources that you need in order to help you bring your commitment into reality. The universe (or God, whichever your belief is) will give you what you need in order to accomplish your goals as long as you have two things: first, a commitment to bringing this goal into your life, and second, the knowledge that it *will* happen; it just hasn't happened *yet*. Having faith is a huge and powerful ingredient in your formula for success.

One Christmas, I took my family to see the Trans-Siberian Orchestra at the Nassau Coliseum in Uniondale, New York. It was a cold and rainy night, but the concert was awesome. If you've never seen this group, even if you don't like rock music, you can't help but love the show that the group puts on. Anyway, when we came out of the concert, it was raining pretty heavily, and I heard somebody outside of my view screaming, "Who needs a hot pretzel?" It was rainy. It was dark. I couldn't see where this voice was coming from. But then I heard it again: "Who needs a hot pretzel?"

I finally turned around, and there was a man standing at the edge of the parking lot with a makeshift grill. It was a grocery shopping cart with coals burning in it, a metal grate across the top, and a bunch of pretzels covered by aluminum foil so that they did not get soaking wet from the rain. I thought to myself, "This is one aggressive man trying to make a living for his family. Kudos to him. He's a hustler. God bless him." But that wasn't the amazing part. What was amazing to me was that there was this long line of people standing there in the cold and the rain, waiting to get *their* hot pretzel. Now, it hadn't been forecast to rain that night, so nobody was prepared. Yet, there these people were, standing in line without umbrellas or raincoats, holding their jackets over their heads to keep dry. They just had to have what he was offering!

Now, you can say that there are a lot of reasons why he was selling so many hot pretzels, but I'm going to tell you what I think. I think it was all about how this man asked the question. You see, he didn't ask, "Does anybody *want* a hot pretzel?" Nor did he say, "I have hot pretzels here." His language was very specific and powerful: "*Who* needs a hot pretzel?" He knew without a shadow of a doubt that people needed what he was selling. He was undeniably certain that with thousands of people coming out of this concert, many of them were absolutely yearning for a hot pretzel—even if they didn't know it yet! And he was confident that he'd find them by shouting out to them through the dark and the rain. *That's faith.* This man came to the concert simply to provide what people were craving. He knew what they wanted, even though they surely hadn't been yearning for a pretzel when they left the building. But when they heard him call, "Who needs a hot pretzel?," it was like a shining beacon through the storm, and the people responded.

When a farmer plants a new crop, there are a lot of things he must do. He has to turn over the soil, add some kind of chemical treatment, plant the seeds, add some fertilizer, water on a regular basis, and then let the sun do its job. I think we can all agree that as the farmer is carrying out all of these activities, he's not saying, "Boy, I hope the seeds grow this time." That farmer knows that when he plants the seeds, they're going to produce a crop. (Note: The farmer represents someone who has supreme faith and KNOWS beyond a shadow of a doubt that what he believes in is true. For the purpose of our discussion, let's assume that in our example we are NOT talking about times of extreme weather events such as floods or drought.)

You should think of your Next Level like the farmer. Don't question whether you're going to reach your Next Level, but have faith that it's going to come to fruition as long as you carry out the right activities that are required of you.

So, have faith that your new life will become your new reality. Your success is certain. In fact, your success already exists. You just need to engage in the right activities to bring it into reality.

There are specific areas of your life that you must address if you hope to get the most out of your abilities and truly design a smile-worthy life. Here are a couple of quick review-style items that you should do to move the ball forward.

Smile Action Steps

* It's important that you do not compare yourself to others. You should compare yourself only to yourself, and how far you've come in your life from where you started. I bet that if you made a list of all the things you have accomplished so far in your life, you would be very proud of yourself. Therefore, please take a moment now and make a list of some of your accomplishments that put a smile on your face. I know there is not enough room for you to write them all, so just write a few that come to mind. (Of course, if you are feeling a little depressed, then get a blank piece of paper and fill it up. If you are *really* depressed, go buy a flip chart and fill that up.) ☺

_____

_____

_____

_____

_____

_____

_____

✳ We know that our health is important, and for some of us, working on this area in our life is the toughest thing to do. There just doesn't seem to be enough "willpower in the bank account" to tackle this area. So, if you were to pick just one thing that you would like to have a breakthrough in, what would that be? What is that one thing that you can commit to doing in the area of health?

_____

_____

_____

_____

_____

_____

_____

✳ What area in your life have you been lacking faith in? The best way to get that faith is by declaring it each and every day. Several times a day would even be better. Here's a simple declaration that you can make: "Thank you (referring to your Higher Power) for giving me the unshakable belief that _____ will come to pass. It is unfolding even now as I speak this sentence. I am ready, willing, and able to receive it. Thank you for giving it to me!" Try that for 30 days, like an experiment, and see if any miracles happen to you.

CHAPTER 11

HOW TO CONQUER FEAR, THE KILLER OF POSSIBILITY

I have learned over the years that when one's mind is made up, this diminishes fear; knowing what must be done does away with fear.

—Rosa Parks

The journey toward achieving your Next Level will not be all peaches and cream. You're going to encounter hurdles along the way, some of which you'll easily clear and others that will most likely trip you up. There will be times when you will want to quit, or when you will feel frustrated or overwhelmed. Here's what you need to know: it's all part of the process.

In other words, it's completely expected that any time you attempt to stretch out of your comfort zone and attain a new goal—particularly if the goal you've targeted is truly a "Next Level" above where you've ever been before—you are going to experience a little turbulence. In fact, you should anticipate that the process won't be pretty at all. Here's the good thing: usually, the bigger the problem, the bigger the breakthrough.

Overcoming Fear

Whenever I think of fear, I am reminded of a particular event that happened when my son was 12 years old. I took him to try out for Little League softball. Now, at this point in my son's life, he was not very athletic. I've never been into sports myself, so I had not encouraged that in him as he was growing up. As the saying goes, the apple doesn't fall far from the tree; however, I had realized that I should try to roll it down the hill just a little bit! Plus, I knew that there were many benefits of being involved in sports that had nothing to do with the game itself.

We showed up at the tryout, and when we walked in, it seemed as if all the other kids were ready to play professional ball. They were wearing their hats, cleats, batting gloves, and other equipment. Michael was wearing jeans and a sweatshirt. He immediately felt embarrassed and wanted to leave. I talked him through it with a little bit of encouragement and got him to stay. Next came a series of tests that would determine the players' ability, and they would be divided into groups based on their performance. Oh, boy, even I was getting uncomfortable.

The first test was the batting cage. As we were standing at the batting cage waiting to go in, the kid that was already in the cage was doing a phenomenal job. He was swinging and hitting every ball. If I had been a baseball scout, I probably would've signed him up for college ball right then. Now, my son was watching this kid and getting more worried as the time passed. You could see the fear starting to take hold of him. At this point, he said to me very clearly: "Dad, I want to go home." I knew that this was probably the most fearful moment he had ever experienced at this point in his 12 years of life. In just a moment, he was going to *walk into a cage, without the protection of his father, while other people judged him.* Can you imagine being thrown into a cage while your peers judged *you*?

So I brought my son over to a bench, sat him down, and said this to him: "Michael, you know what I do for a living, that I help adults learn how to be more successful in their life." He responded, "Yes, Daddy." I continued, "I'm going to tell you the number one thing that holds adults back from being truly happy and successful in their life. **They don't have fear . . . fear has them.** So, Michael, I want you to go into that cage, and I don't care whether you hit the ball or not. I just don't want fear to hold you back from playing in life." And, wouldn't you know? The awesome kid that my son is, he just looked at me and said. "OK, Daddy."

Michael went into the cage, *with* his fear, and swung the bat. He hit some balls and missed a lot of them, and then went on to do the other tests—pitching, running, and catching. After about 90 minutes of running around and playing, my son came and sat next to me on the bench. He was a little sweaty and a lot tired.

"Thanks, Dad. I had fun today," he said. I told him, "I'm so proud of you. I don't want you to forget this. It's OK to have fear, but don't let fear have you. Don't let fear hold you back from playing in life. Have the fear . . . and swing anyway."

What's really important is not whether we succeed or not, because at the end of it all, most of us will be contemplating not the *quantity* of our life but the *quality* of it. We won't regret the things that we *have* done as much as we regret the things that we *haven't* done. Fear robs us of taking risks and playing full out in life.

Let's look at another example. In my years of corporate training and coaching, one of the industries that I've focused on is sales. And one of the biggest challenges that most salespeople have is prospecting. Whether it's on the telephone or door-to-door, the thing that stops most salespeople is fear. In helping salespeople to overcome their fear, I ask them to answer this question: "What are you committed to accomplishing with this prospect?" (Now, as an aside, most salespeople will say, "To close the lead," but I coach them that this is wrong; what they should really be committed to is building a relationship with the prospect. If you build a relationship with someone, you will naturally do business with that person. But I digress.)

The point here is that either we are focused on our thoughts, feelings, and concerns—in other words, our fear—or we are focused on what we're committed to accomplishing. So, the bottom line, just as I told Michael by the batting cages, is to *take the fear with you* and take action anyway. Do the thing that allows you to fulfill your commitment—in this case, building a relationship with a potential customer.

FEAR: False Evidence Appearing Real

This is just a little acronym that helps me remember that fear is "nothing to be afraid of."

Fear is a chemical occurrence in your brain, and it has nothing to do with what's actually happening outside your head. So to a large extent, when we fear something, it's something that we are making up. It's not real.

Back in the seventeenth century and earlier, when a cartographer (mapmaker) wanted to mark an area on a map where the waters had not yet been charted, he would put dragons there. Some people would see the dragons on the map and say, "Oh, no, uncharted areas. Let's stay away." Others would see them and say, "Oh, boy, uncharted territories! Let's go check them out!" You may have some uncharted areas in your life, things that seem scary. But I say that's where the real opportunities are. Fear is not something to run away from; it's something to embrace. Fear makes life all that much more exciting when you push through it and experience something new. So don't run from your dragons—run toward them.

What really causes fear (aside from chemicals in our brain) is not knowing something that hasn't occurred yet. Because we don't know what may or may not happen, we feel unstable. But let's consider the meaning of *possibility*. Is possibility something that you already have? Is it something that you already know how to do? Isn't possibility something that hasn't happened yet, that you don't know how to do yet, and where you really don't know what the end result will be? Fear and possibility are closely related, but when you live from fear, you don't move toward possibility—and if you don't move toward possibility, you're going to stay stagnant, never attaining your Next Level.

The obvious benefit to pushing through your fear is that you might accomplish something great in your life. But another great benefit, whether or not you reach your goals, is the fact that your fear did not control you—instead, you controlled your fear. That in and of itself provides a huge sense of accomplishment, which empowers you to take more risks and challenges in your life.

I was in a pizza parlor with my son and his friend Chuck. While we were sitting at the table, we saw this little six-year-old girl waiting with her mother as they ordered pizza. But this girl wasn't just waiting. She was humming and dancing, singing and twirling around, right in the middle of the floor. As we watched her, I said to Michael and Chuck, "When we get older in life, we don't dare dance in public."

Chuck's response was, "Well, she hasn't learned fear yet, or embarrassment."

I couldn't resist asking, "So, what would life look like without fear and embarrassment?" He answered, "You'd probably take more risks and do a lot more, and you'd dance in public."

I think Chuck nailed it. Remember how you were as a child? You would take more risks and not think twice about them. As a matter of fact, you didn't see things as "risks" at all. You were too young to have "learned" how to be afraid or embarrassed. It was just about you playing and having fun in life.

I bet one of the reasons that a lot of us enjoy going to parties or weddings is that it gives us permission to dance in public. How would you feel if you danced in public for no reason? What if, while you waited on the supermarket line, you just started to do a little shuffle? What if, instead of walking to your car, you actually skipped? Besides the short workout, I have a feeling that it might also put a smile on your face—and on the faces of the other people watching you.

You have to remember that fear and embarrassment are emotions that are going to happen automatically. But they can be overcome. If you want to live a life worth smiling about, it's absolutely essential that you live from possibilities, not from fear.

Smile Action Steps

* *What's the worst thing that can happen?* A great way to deal with your fear is to consider the worst-case scenario. Really get specific and look at the worst possible thing that can happen in the situation you're afraid of (for example, someone will laugh at you if you dance while you're waiting for pizza, or your boss

will say no if you request a raise). Then ask yourself if you can live through that potentially negative situation. If you decide that you can, there are several results that you'll achieve right off the bat. First, if the worst-case scenario does occur, you're already prepared for it mentally. Therefore, you'll survive it just fine. Second, just by going through the exercise of thinking about living through the worst-case scenario, you'll find that the fear inside you is lessened—which then makes you more able to get into action and move toward the thing that you want to accomplish. Again, fear is mostly about not knowing what's going to happen. By mentally rehearsing the worst-case scenario, you'll feel stronger. But here's the best part about this process: nine times out of ten, the worst-case scenario doesn't happen. So, when all is said and done, your reaction is likely to be something like, "Boy, that wasn't so bad after all." Make a list of a few things that you have been afraid to do and write the worst-case scenario for each to see if you can live through it.

_____

_____

_____

_____

_____

_____

_____

❋ *Do it anyway.* The next time you're about to do something that makes you uncomfortable and these fearful feelings start to creep up on you, here's my suggestion. Let your brain do what it always does, which is to react in a chemical way (causing what we perceive as fear), and then simply *take action anyway.* In other words, bring that fear with you and take action toward the *thing that you are committed to* doing. Tony Robbins said it best when he said, "Motion impacts emotion." Eventually, by taking action even when you are afraid, you will conquer that fear, and it won't be as strong next time.

* *Change your language.* I want you to try this simple technique. The next time you're fearful of something, mentally swap out the word *afraid* and instead insert the word *excited*. The chemical reaction inside of us and the "butterflies in our stomachs" are identical for both emotions—it's just our interpretation that shifts. So, let's say you have to make a presentation in front of your coworkers. Instead of telling yourself, "I'm *afraid* to speak in front of these people," try, "I'm *excited* to speak in front of these people!" Keep repeating the more positive interpretation to yourself and you'll notice how your feelings begin to shift. In the following chart, I would like you to list three things that you would like to accomplish in your life, but that your fear is holding you back from. Write the fear statement next to each, and then rewrite the statement replacing the fear with excitement.

Item to Accomplish	Fear Statement	Excited Statement

CHAPTER 12

A SETBACK IS A SETUP FOR A COMEBACK

Discovery consists of seeing what everybody has seen and thinking what nobody has thought.

—Albert Szent-Györgyi, *biochemist (1893–1986)*

Obstacles in our path may be opportunities to improve our condition. There is an old fable that talks about a king in ancient times who purposely placed a boulder on a roadway. He then hid himself and watched to see whether anyone would remove the huge rock. Some of the wealthiest merchants and courtiers of the kingdom came by and simply walked around the boulder. Many of them loudly blamed the king for not keeping the roads clear, but none of them did anything about getting the stone out of the way. Then a peasant came along carrying a load of vegetables. Upon approaching the boulder, the peasant laid down his burden and tried to move the stone to the side of the road. After much pushing and straining, he finally succeeded. When the peasant picked up his load of vegetables, he noticed a purse lying in the road where the boulder had been. The purse contained many gold coins and a note from the king indicating that the gold was for the person who removed the boulder from the roadway. The peasant learned that every obstacle presents an opportunity to improve our condition.

Traditionally, when we have a problem, we think that the best approach is to figure out how to solve it. But what if we approached each problem as an opportunity?

Four Ways to Look at Problems as Opportunities

Solving a problem does not necessarily create growth. When you look at a problem as an opportunity, however, what you end up with is not just a solution to the problem, but actually an improvement in the quality of your life. So, when you are faced with a problem, the question to ask yourself is, "What is the opportunity here, and how can I grow from this experience?"

1. "Half Empty" Is a Good Thing

You've all heard the expression about the glass being half empty or half full. The idea is that we should have a more positive outlook and "look on the bright side," which presumably is seeing the glass as half full. But I am going to turn that old expression on its head. Check it out.

If you take a glass that already has something in it, you can't do anything about what's already in the glass. Actually, the empty space in the glass is where possibility exists. Focusing on the glass as half empty gives you the freedom and opportunity to create, to invent something that works better for you than the current situation. Of course, it's important that we appreciate (with gratitude) what we have in our life, but it's what we *don't* have—what might seem "missing," the empty part of the glass—that provides us with the fantastic opportunity to design our Next Level.

2. Trust That Bad Things May Be for Your Own Good

As we discussed earlier in this book, when things go wrong and you think the universe is working against you, that's when it's most important to have faith. Here's a story you'll enjoy. My Uncle Jack and Aunt Nancy had this car they called "Old Betsy." Now, Old Betsy always seemed to have mechanical problems (the word *old* should be a clue as to why). My uncle, being a devout Roman Catholic, would even pray that his car would be taken care of and that it would stop breaking down every other week. Still, Betsy broke down again and again, and it was always pretty expensive to fix. Eventually, Old Betsy "died."

My uncle and aunt were very upset at the time, as they were now forced to travel to work by bus. After a couple weeks of this new routine, they couldn't take it anymore, so they went to the car dealership. They chose this brand-new, wonderful, all-the-bells-and-whistles car. My uncle called me after the purchase and told me how concerned he was about the payments and whether he could afford the new car. I asked him to think back and tell me how much money he and my aunt had been spending on Old Betsy by trying to repair her for the previous two years. It turned out that the monthly payment for the new car was *20 percent less* a year than what they had been spending to try to keep Old Betsy alive.

So here's what I said to my uncle. "For two years, Uncle Jack, you prayed for your car. And though it didn't seem like it, your prayers were in fact answered every time the car broke down. It just wasn't the answer you were looking for. It was like God was saying, 'That pain in the butt, Jack. How many times do I have to make Betsy break down before he takes the hint and gets a new car?'" So I pointed out to Uncle Jack that if he had followed the signs, learned the lesson, and gotten rid of the car earlier, he probably would have saved himself a lot of aggravation, saved a lot of money, and had a new car two years sooner to boot!

So, here's the point. If you have faith that what you're committed to is going to become reality, when it starts to look as if the universe is working against you, it may actually be working *for* you. You have to pay attention to the signs. The universe will always give you what you need as long as you're truly committed to recognizing and accepting the signs when they show themselves.

I'm going to mention one other example here that may be a little sensitive. With great sadness I remember our national tragedy that took place on September 11, 2001. When airplanes flew into and took down the two buildings of the World Trade Center in New York City that morning, causing nearly 3,000 deaths, there were a number of individuals who *would have been* among the casualties, but weren't because of what seemed like a random twist of fate.[1] Some of these "near misses" were caused by casual decisions that the individual made; in other cases, the people involved were initially frustrated or annoyed by circumstances that had caused them not to be where they wanted to be at that time. There was the head chef at the Windows on the World restaurant, located on floors 106 and 107 of One World Trade Center, who at the last minute switched his eyeglass repair appointment from noon that day to 8:00 a.m. and wound up in the lobby of the building rather than upstairs at his desk when disaster struck . . . the flight attendant who accidentally inverted two code numbers in the airline's system and wound up being assigned to a different flight . . . the wealthy property developer whose wife insisted that he not miss his doctor's appointment (as he had intended to that morning) and who therefore was not in the building when the planes hit.

In each of these instances, people's lives were literally saved by what seemed like a chance occurrence or by some inconvenient interruption of their day. So, the next time you're caught in traffic, or when somebody bumps into you and wants to have a long conversation, making you late for an important meeting, trust in the fact that the universe may be lining up certain things for your benefit to help you achieve the very thing that you are committed to bringing into your life, or to prevent you from encountering something negative. Trust that whatever is happening is *exactly* what needs to happen for your good fortune.

3. Keep Smiling!

Let's not forget to approach our problems with a smile. We already know that when we smile, it helps reduce our stress and our blood pressure, which of course means that we can solve our problems with more energy and creativity. So, keep smiling in the face of your problems.

Here's a really fun example of how smiling can lift your spirits and help keep you firmly on the road to success. Michelle Jenneke is a hurdler from Australia who won a silver medal for the 100-meter hurdles at the 2010 Summer Youth Olympics, along with many other medals in various competitions. In 2012, she became a media sensation when a video of her warm-up routine at the 100-meter hurdles race at the 2012 World Junior Championships in Athletics in Barcelona went viral. *Hmmm. How do I explain this?* Let's just say that before starting to run, Michelle has a smile from ear to ear, she jumps up and down enthusiastically, she does a little dance—for minutes on end. All the while, her competitors are going through the process of warming themselves up—very serious, focused, and taking deep breaths. You can't keep your eyes off Michelle, though, because her excitement and joy are just contagious. (In fact, I dare you to watch the video and not smile yourself!)

The bottom line is that while at first it might appear a little over-the-top and odd to watch an accomplished athlete who is so giddy before an event, the results speak for themselves. Once the starting gun sounds, Michelle takes off like a lightning bolt and literally blows away the competition. Then she effortlessly comes to a stop and—smiling as broadly as ever—goes to congratulate the other hurdlers. I posted this clip on my Facebook page and got tons of comments. It's really amazing to see. And it's impossible not to feed off her energy. I encourage you to go ahead and search for her online; you'll see what I'm talking about. And while you're watching her, imagine what would happen if you brought that level of joy and ease to *your* life! What could you accomplish if your smile and your love for what you do were so overwhelming that you just couldn't keep them to yourself? Maybe you'd notch a few more wins, just like Michelle.

4. Don't Be a Victim

Be careful of your "stinkin' thinkin'." If the problem you're currently facing seems like it was done *to* you, resist the temptation to play the victim role. As we've said, problems are our opportunity to improve our lives. So don't look at what was done *to* you, but rather look at what is being done *for* you. Your setback is a setup for a comeback.

You've probably heard the saying, "When one door closes, another opens," right? The full quote, actually, is from Alexander Graham Bell, and I think it is very powerful: "When one door closes, another door opens; but we so often look so long and regretfully upon the closed door, that we do not see the ones which open for us." So, what does this mean? I think it means that regardless of what happens to you, accept that it happened for a reason (which may at the time be difficult to understand) and look for a way to "turn lemons into lemonade."

A friend of mine recently left a company that he had cofounded only a few years earlier. The business was starting to pick up steam, but he and his partner had some differences of opinion, and rather than lose the friendship entirely, he decided that it was best for him to move on. However, he didn't have an actual exit strategy, so he literally left his position and walked headlong into nothingness. He had no income. No immediate prospects. And an angry wife. However, within just a few short months, and without really hitting the phones or knocking on tons of doors, he turned his career around. He teamed up with a few colleagues in similar fields and brought in business. Old clients called him from seemingly out of nowhere when they heard about his availability. And within a few months, he had earned more than he had done the entire previous year.

How did this happen for my friend? I say (and he agrees) that it's because he didn't wallow in anger toward his former partner, focus on his regrets, or become depressed about his current situation. He refused to be a victim. Instead, he looked forward and committed to creating something better for himself and his family. And he accomplished just that.

Problems Make You Stronger

As you start to work toward your Next Level and design a life worth smiling about, you're going to face challenges. Sometimes you may think they're bigger than you can handle. Let me share some thoughts to help you through that.

Take a moment to think of a previous challenge in your life, a really difficult one, a problem or situation that seemed like there was no way you would get through it. As a matter of fact, at the time, it was the absolute worst moment you had had in your life up to that point. You had no idea how you were going to deal with it, or why it was happening to you. You felt almost hopeless. My question is: did you get through it?

It may not have been easy, but I'm going to guess that you made it through to the other side. Not only did you get through it, but today you are even stronger because of it, and you probably took away some valuable lessons. My point is that if you were able to get through that particular situation, then you'll get through any problems or challenges that you're facing right now.

Carrot, Egg, or Coffee Bean?

There is a story about a mother who invited her daughter into the kitchen to discuss some problems that the daughter was having. When they arrived in the kitchen, the mother already had three pots of water boiling on the stove. Lying on the counter were a pile of fresh carrots, some eggs, and some coffee beans. She sat her daughter down and proceeded to take each pile of items and put it in its own pot of boiling water. After about 20 minutes, she turned off the burners and fished out the carrots, placing them in a bowl. Then she pulled out the eggs and placed them in a bowl. And, finally, she took out the coffee beans in their liquid and placed them in their own bowl.

The mother then asked her daughter to feel the carrots. She did so and noted that they were soft. The mother then asked the daughter to take an egg and break it. After pulling off the shell, the daughter observed the hard-boiled egg. Finally, the mother asked the daughter to sip the coffee. The daughter tasted its richness and savored its aroma.

She then asked, "What does this mean, mother?" Her mother explained that each of these objects had faced the same adversity—boiling water. But each had reacted differently. The carrot went in strong, hard, and unyielding. However, after being subjected to the boiling water, it softened and became weak. The egg had been fragile. Its thin outer shell had protected its liquid interior, but after sitting in the boiling water, its inside became hardened. The coffee beans were unique, however. While they were being boiled, they had changed the water.

"Which are you?" she asked her daughter. "When adversity knocks on your door, how do you respond? Are you a carrot, an egg, or a coffee bean?"

You may know people who have been through so much adversity that it has actually weakened their spirit, making them soft like the carrot after boiling for 20 minutes. You may know others who after so many challenges have become hard inside and don't allow other people to win their hearts. But the most blessed people are those who are like coffee beans. From the challenges and adversities that they go through, they transform themselves to the point where they actually make the outside world, their water, different from what it was before the challenge that they faced. Also, the challenge brings out their flavor and their best aroma. I say that we should all be more like coffee beans—

not only becoming stronger, but having the ability to help others and to transform the world that surrounds you.

Keep in mind that when you face a major challenge, you will naturally focus more on that area of your life than on others. When you concentrate your energy, it also makes you stronger in that particular area. It's just like when you go to the gym and focus on certain muscles, those muscles will get stronger.

A colleague of mine used to work on his own in the marketing field, and then went to work for an advertising agency. When he first started there, he didn't understand the proper timing of working with copywriters, designers, web developers, and other such professionals. He was so used to doing everything himself that he hadn't learned the skill of how to delegate. The art department would regularly complain to management that he was submitting concepts too late and jamming them up. Things got pretty tense. It took almost a full year, but he eventually got the hang of "feeding the pipeline" properly, and he became one of the firm's top producers over the next five years. He had survived under pressure, adapted his behavior, and thrived.

What Peter Taught Me

Most races are won in the last quarter mile. I remember one time I was on a skiing trip with my son and his friends, and we decided to have a race down the mountain. We were halfway down, and I was tied with my son and his friend Peter. Peter wiped out, and I wound up passing my son. So at this point I was now in the lead, and I was giggling, knowing that this old man was beating all these young studs. I was 100 yards from the "finish line," and I was positive that I was going to beat everybody. But I made a fatal error. I decided to coast the rest of the way, and about 50 yards from the base of the mountain, I heard Peter screaming with joy as he passed me, ultimately beating me in our race. When we were all back at the lodge reviewing our "Olympic" competition, I asked the boys what we could learn from this. Here's what we all agreed we learned: (1) that a race isn't over until it's over, so don't slow down until you've won; and (2) that even if it seems as though you've wiped out, stay persistent and don't give up and you can still win the race.

You May Fail More Than You Succeed

A good friend of mine, Steve Harney, enjoys just about any form of sports. Steve recently taught me something about baseball. One of the stats that signifies a level of excellence for baseball players is if they are able to hit the ball and reach base safely three times out of ten opportunities while batting. Put another way, when a batter *fails* seven out of ten times, he can still be a Hall of Famer. When Steve told me this, it blew my mind. What if the baseball player got depressed and quit because he failed those seven times? The lesson here is to keep grinding away. It doesn't necessarily take a lot of success to transform your life, but you mustn't quit.

The Emperor Moth

A man found a cocoon of an Emperor moth. He took it home so that he could watch the moth come out of the cocoon. One day, a small opening appeared, and the man sat and watched the moth for several hours as it struggled to force its body through that little hole. Then the moth seemed to stop making any progress, as if it had gotten as far as it could and could go no farther. It appeared to be stuck. So, the man, in his kindness, decided to help the moth. He took a pair of scissors and snipped off the remaining bit of the cocoon. The moth then emerged easily. But it had a swollen body and small, shriveled wings. The man continued to watch the moth because he expected that at any moment, the wings would enlarge and expand so that they would be able to support the body, which, he assumed, would contract in time. But neither happened!

In fact, the little moth spent the rest of its life crawling around with a swollen body and shriveled wings. It was never able to fly. What the man in his kindness and haste did not understand was that the restricting cocoon and the struggle required for the moth to get through the tiny opening were nature's way of forcing fluid from the moth's body into its wings so that it would be ready for flight once it achieved its freedom from the cocoon. Freedom and flight would come only after the struggle. By depriving the moth of this struggle, he inadvertently deprived it of it's ability to fly. Sometimes struggles are exactly what we need in our life. If we were to go through our life without any obstacles, we would be crippled. We would not be as strong as we could have been.

Learn from Your Mistakes

There is an old adage that goes, "Success is the worst teacher, because you learn only from your mistakes." Most of us look at mistakes and challenges as a bad thing, when in fact, it's our mistakes that help us learn to improve. There is a story I heard once about a ceramics teacher who announced on opening day that he was dividing the class into two groups. All those on the left side of the studio, he said, would be graded solely on the quantity of the work they produced; all those on the right side would be graded solely on its quality. His procedure was simple: on the final day of class, he would bring in his bathroom scales and weigh the work of the "quantity" group. Those being graded on quality, however, needed to produce only one pot—albeit a perfect one—to get an A. Well, grading time came, and a curious fact emerged: the highest-quality works were all produced by the group that was being graded on quantity. It seems that while the quantity group was busily churning out piles of work (and learning from its mistakes), the quality group had sat theorizing about perfection, and in the end had little more to show for its efforts than grandiose theories and a pile of dead clay.

The lesson here is that taking action and being willing to fail is the quickest route to success. True, you may not be perfect in whatever you do—whether it's a business project, a personal relationship, or even playing sports—but if you think about it all day (or longer) and never actually "get in the game," you'll have little to show for it. Are you one of those people who suffers from "paralysis by analysis"? If so, unless it's a matter of life and death, the best thing to do is to make a decision and give it a try. You can always correct your course once you break the inertia and get moving.

Smile Action Steps

 ❋ *Recognize that the problem itself is never the problem; rather, the problem is your thoughts about the problem.* As we said earlier, and it bears repeating, stress, fear, and anxiety are all chemical reactions in our brain based on learned responses to previous situations. When we start to look at the facts of our life, remember that what we say is a problem is really our perception of what's happening, and we're calling this a problem. If the problem is really a made-up thought in our brain about the facts of our life, then we have the ability to reprogram our thinking and look at the issue not as a problem but as an opportunity. Ask yourself, what new thoughts can I have about my current challenges?

_____

_____

_____

_____

_____

_____

_____

* *Be flexible in your thinking.* We can all learn a lesson from the trees. The trees that are left standing after a big storm are the ones that were able to bend when the wind came through. The ones that were rigid and inflexible are usually the ones that you see down on the ground. They couldn't handle the storm. Either they snapped, or they got completely uprooted. Remember to be flexible through the storms that you may get hit with. There's something especially interesting about a palm tree. It's been said that a palm tree's roots actually get stronger in a hurricane.

* *Ask yourself,* "What can I learn from this challenge?" Like we said, problems are not something that are done *to us*, but rather things that are done *for us*. In every challenging situation, there's a learning opportunity for us to develop a new skill that

we'll be able to use in our day-to-day lives. What can you learn from your current challenge now?

_____

_____

_____

_____

_____

_____

_____

* *Be persistent and don't give up.* If we think of the story about me skiing with my son's friends, and what Peter taught me, the race is not over until it's over. You need to pick yourself up and finish the race. So what area in your life have you given up in, where perhaps you should pick yourself up and finish the race?

_____

_____

_____

_____

_____

_____

_____

* *Train your brain to focus on the things that support your getting to your Next Level.*

Have you ever wondered how sports referees are able to see so many things during the course of a football game? They can do it because their assignment is to focus on a very specific set of actions. No single official can watch everything. So, instead, one official watches the quarterback. Another runs with the receivers. A different one zeroes in on the offensive and defensive lines. By paying attention to only a narrow area on the field of play, they can achieve their goal of properly officiating the game. Think of yourself as a referee with a trained eye and a singular focus on seeking out anything that can help you—and disregarding the rest.

* *Don't waste your time complaining.* When you focus on your current problem, all it does is mentally and physically drain you (not to mention the fact that it doesn't bring you any closer to moving forward in your life). You should always be thinking about what's going to help you move forward in your life. What actions are you going to take that will bring you closer to your Next Level? What complaint have you had for a while that you are always willing to share with whoever is willing to listen to you? Write it here, and then make a commitment to leave it in the pages of this book and never verbally repeat it to anyone ever again. Don't worry if you miss it . . . you can always come back to this page and read it to yourself.

_____

_____

_____

_____

_____

_____

_____

CHAPTER 13

TURNING BREAKDOWNS INTO BREAKTHROUGHS

Adversity reveals genius; prosperity conceals it.

—Horace

What's the difference between a problem and a breakdown? Well, if you think of a problem or a challenge as a speed bump in the road, then you should think of a breakdown as a roadblock, something preventing you from going any farther. You're at a complete standstill. It seems as if there is nowhere for you to turn, and you are stuck.

For instance, if you wanted a promotion at work and someone else from your department was named to the position ahead of you, that's a breakdown. If you fight with your spouse every single time you bring up your child's college education, that's a breakdown.

Just as with problems, however, there is opportunity here. Breakdowns, when dealt with productively, can produce *breakthroughs*.

Breakdowns

In the armed services back in the 1950s and 1960s, before flight simulators, test pilots would take a new piece of equipment and push it beyond its limitations with the intention of deliberately producing a breakdown in the machinery. As you can imagine, this was a risky job.

When pilots found breakdowns in the machinery, they would use this information to determine the overall performance of the aircraft. This overall performance was the breakthrough. Today, software firms hire computer "hackers" to deliberately try to crash their systems. These companies are intentionally trying to create a breakdown of their own making, so that they can expose their own weaknesses and better design their product.

Now, in your life, most of the breakdowns that will occur are likely to take place without your purposely planning for them. For instance, you might have something that you're trying to produce in the area of money, health, or relationships, and it seems as if you keep hitting a major roadblock that's preventing you from moving forward. So what do you do?

Breakthrough Thinking

When you find yourself blocked, filled with negative thoughts, and feeling like you're stuck, there are some specific steps to take to achieve a life-changing breakthrough.

Take Responsibility

In order for you to be the cause of your life instead of the effect of it, whenever there is a breakdown, you have to look to *see where you're responsible*. What is it that *you* did or did not do that caused this breakdown? Don't get me wrong; I'm not talking about your blaming yourself or feeling like a victim. The point is to take responsibility so that you can then do what's needed to fix the situation and get back on track.

There's a fable that goes something like this: a man went to a Zen Buddhist monk to figure out how he could lessen the problems in his life. The Buddhist monk was sitting in front of a lake, and he asked the gentleman to pick up a pebble and throw it in the water. The pebble splashed in and created ripples, which the monk asked the man to stop. So the man put his hand in the lake; however, in doing so, instead of stopping the ripples, he only created more. The man looked at the monk and told him that it would be impossible to stop the ripples. The monk said to him, "How you stop the ripple is that you don't throw the pebble into the lake in the first place."

Most of the challenges and ripples that we have in our lives occur because somewhere, somehow, we threw the pebble. This is true whether we did so intentionally or not, or even whether we believe that it was or was not our "fault." The point is, when you have a breakdown, you need to purposely take responsibility for having created this issue in the first place. By doing so, you'll acknowledge your own role in the situation, and, rather than being a victim at the mercy of external circumstances beyond your control, you'll mentally accept the idea that if you have the power to cause the problem to begin with, you naturally have the power to find the solution. Thus, by taking responsibility for the underlying issue, you are granting yourself the power to also create the breakthrough that you need.

Separate Your Thoughts from the Facts

As I said earlier, what happens in our life (the facts) is separate from what we think, feel, and believe about what happened. What we think, feel, and believe is an automatic, trained response that has nothing to do with the reality of what actually occurred. When we train our brain to distinguish between these two areas, we can look at the breakdown more objectively and become less emotional about it.

Remember, the emotional hurricane that we create in our own minds can make a breakdown much worse. Our emotions cloud our thinking and judgment about what needs to happen next if we are to have a breakthrough. This is why it's so important to distinguish the reality of what happened from our thoughts, feelings, and opinions about what happened. When you separate the two, you can deal directly with the facts and be effective.

Ask Yourself What You're Committed To

Use this breakdown as an opportunity to clarify what it is that you're committed to accomplishing. If you weren't committed to producing a particular result—whether in your business, your relationships, or your life in general—this thing that happened wouldn't seem like a breakdown in the first place. It's only because the result is important to you that not having it becomes a problem. For example, if you weren't committed to advancing your career, the fact that you didn't receive a promotion wouldn't be a big deal. If you are committed to your career, however, not receiving that promotion would be devastating. Therefore, the breakdown actually validates what you are committed to.

Recommit

Even with clarity concerning your commitments, you won't have a breakthrough without taking action to reach these goals. The key word here is *action.* Let's take a look at this diagram.

In the center, you have what I'm calling a breakdown. As I said earlier, you can choose to look at the breakdown based on your thoughts, feelings, and opinions, and then make a decision, or you can look at the breakdown based on what you're committed to and take action based on that. Obviously, if you take action based on your thoughts, feelings, and opinions, you're going to wind up simply validating your own preconceived notions. For example, your thoughts might go something like this: "Training for a marathon is difficult. I don't like getting up at 4 a.m., and I definitely don't like how much my calves hurt. So, I'll quit." Then, you would automatically think, "See? I knew I'd never be a runner anyway." But if you take action based on your commitment, your mind will seek out evidence to validate that. "I'm committed to running in order to raise money for a charity that means a lot to me. Yes, it's painful, inconvenient, and uncomfortable, but I'll find a way to do it!"

Ask Yourself What You Learned from This Experience

Every breakdown is an opportunity for you to learn. Without learning, a breakdown is just a waste of time. I spoke earlier about test pilots pushing a plane beyond its limitations in order to find a breakdown in the machinery of the plane. If they did this and then ignored their own findings, the exercise would be not only a waste of time, but a waste of life! So, the whole purpose is to learn and improve from the breakdown. Ask yourself how you can avoid this same negative scenario next time. How can you push forward to reach your goal? If you can walk away from a breakdown as a stronger human being, then it was a lesson well learned.

Why Breakdowns Occur

I believe that challenges and breakdowns occur for one of two reasons. First, sometimes the universe is testing your commitment and resolve to see whether you are truly committed. Therefore, it throws obstacles in your way, creates challenges, and tests you. Almost everyone who has accomplished great things in their life will tell you that they did it while facing extreme challenges. People who say that they are committed, but in their heart truly aren't, quickly give up when they are faced with a breakdown. Remember, your breakdown is a test to see whether you are serious about your commitment.

The second reason why I believe you have breakdowns is that the universe is trying to prepare you to receive the abundance that you are about to receive. I mean, think about it. If you're committed to having a life-altering accomplishment, you have to be ready for it. It's like somebody who wins a multimillion-dollar lottery. Studies show that many lottery winners soon lose all the money that they won. Why? Because they mentally and emotionally were not ready to receive it. It sort of came out of nowhere, and they didn't have the preparation to develop the proper habits they needed if they were to hold onto their newfound wealth and make it grow.

Therefore, the trials and tribulations that we go through are actually training and conditioning us to be able to effectively handle the new-found abundance that will occur in our lives. So, bring on the break-downs! Keep on smiling, learning, and producing breakthroughs on the road to your Next Level.

The Anatomy of an Upset

In any situation that causes you to be upset, there are likely to be one of three causes: unfulfilled expectations, undelivered communications, or thwarted intentions. Let's take a brief look at each one. Being able to identify the upset is half the battle in avoiding it altogether.

Unfulfilled Expectations

Take a look at all your relationships—whether with family members, friends, or acquaintances—and honestly examine the times when they've disappointed you. Or, examine any work situation where you became upset over something that occurred, or that didn't occur. Chances are that you had expectations that weren't fulfilled. I'm talking about expecting certain results from somebody based on your own values, thoughts, and opinions, without necessarily having worked with the other person to make sure that what you wanted to have come about was actually in the works. For instance, maybe you expected your significant other to buy you something for a key anniversary, and he didn't. Or perhaps you expected your supervisor to offer you a pat on the back after you worked all weekend on a report. Maybe you even expected a raise or a promotion for your efforts. When our preconceived desires don't turn out the way we anticipated, we're in for a letdown.

On the other hand, if you're careful to be aware of what you expect from others and, in fact, to guard against setting expectations that you leave uncommunicated (see the next section), you'll find that you'll be more receptive to (and happier with) the actual actions that others take. You'll start to appreciate other people more, and just the slightest things that they do will put a smile on your face.

Undelivered Communications

Have you ever had somebody important in your life do something that upset you, but you decided not to say anything because you were hoping that your feelings would go away or get better? Or perhaps you believe internally that you're not justified in thinking or feeling a certain way and that it would be silly to say anything, so you just suppress your feelings? Let me tell you what actually happens when we take this route: that little thought or feeling that you think is going to go away by itself actually gets bigger and stronger.

So, what should you do with this undelivered communication? You need to deliver it. You need to calmly and effectively share with your loved one what's on your mind. In doing this, though, it's important that you don't have an expectation, which we spoke about earlier, that this person will do something about this thought or feeling that you have. It's also important that you don't use this opportunity to blame the person for something. Rather, by simply communicating, it's a way for you to clear this thought and feeling from your brain and get it out of your head, removing it as an obstacle for you and the other person.

Thwarted Intentions

If you attempt to do something and, for whatever reason, it just doesn't work out, that can be quite upsetting, right? An easy example to illustrate this is if you were working as part of a project team in your office to solicit feedback from employees about a new product launch. You came into the office on Monday all gung ho about ideas that you came up with over the weekend on how to implement this initiative—only to learn that upper management had shifted the direction of the project and your work could not be put to use. This would certainly be frustrating. Remember, the key here, as I mentioned earlier, is simply to become aware of what it is that is causing you to be upset.

The next time you are upset, pay attention to which of the three scenarios—unfulfilled expectations, undelivered communications, or thwarted intentions—is driving you. Recognizing this will better enable you to communicate with those in your life and move the action forward toward something positive.

Stress

We often use the term *stressed out* to describe how we're feeling. But, what is stress really? As of November 25, 2013, the website for the American Institute of Stress states, "Stress is not a useful term for scientists because it is such a highly subjective phenomenon that it defies definition." If you were to ask 10 different people to describe stress, you'd get 10 different answers. It's one of those things that's difficult to define, but everybody knows what you're talking about when you say it.

Think about something that you are *stressed* about right now. It could be a relationship that you're currently in, your finances, or even an exam at school. To help you learn how to approach a stressful situation, we're going back to the distinction we spoke about earlier when we used the example of *Apollo 13*. There was the explosion, which was a fact, and then there was the "box," which was full of our *automatic thoughts*. Let's now break a stressful situation into those same two parts: the fact of what is actually happening and your thoughts and feelings *about* what's happening.

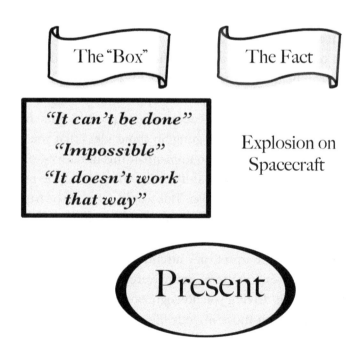

Let's say you have $500 in your checkbook and you have $1,000 in bills to pay. This might seem like a silly question, but here goes: "Is that a problem?" Your knee-jerk reaction might be, "Of course it is!"

The truth is, having $500 in your checkbook and $1,000 worth of bills to pay is simply a *fact*. It is the current state of your finances, that's all. Now let's look at some of the possible *thoughts and feelings* you might have about your checkbook: "Where am I going to get the extra $500?" "Am I going to start getting calls from bill collectors?" "What would people think of me if they knew this?" "I feel like such a loser!" And so on.

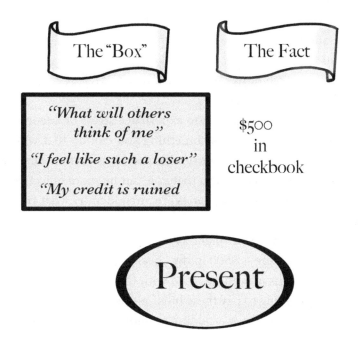

Consider these feelings, and now think about what is *actually* stressing you out. Is it the *fact* that you have only $500 in your checkbook, or is it your *thoughts and feelings* about the $500 in your checkbook? The fact remains that you do not have enough money to cover your expenses, so paying your bills is obviously going to be a real challenge.

But, now tell me this: Would you be much more effective at solving this challenge if you considered your options in a clear-headed state? Will the angst and drama that you are about to put yourself through help you in any way to get these bills paid? Absolutely not. What they may get you is high blood pressure, and possibly even an ulcer over time. Once again, it is your inner thoughts that are taking over and steering you off course—your perceptions about your reality create your stress.

Imagine one of those abstract paintings where it looks as if the painter splashed different-colored paint all over a canvas. You can have one person see it and say that the piece looks like two doves drinking coffee, while another person will see two penguins dancing on a cake. That painting will appear different based on the individual's interpretation. There are objective facts about the painting (the colors and the canvas), and then there are our interpretations. Similarly, we have facts about our lives (money in our checkbook, for instance), and then we have our interpretations. We live from our interpretations as if they were truly the facts of our lives.

So the next time you start to experience stress or become worried, upset, or freaked out, here's something you can do that will help you make a good decision and deal with the stress better. First, separate the facts from your feelings so that you can be more objective. A great technique is to state what the *facts* are, then identify what you're *feeling* about the facts.

So, for example, you might say: "The fact is that I have $1,000 in bills to pay, and there is $500 in my checking account. The feelings that come up, which have nothing to do with the facts, are that I'm worried about how I'm going to pay these bills." Notice that I did not say, "I have *only* $500." The word *only* is adding opinion to the fact. The fact has no emotion to it. It is what it is.

Remember that our thoughts and feelings come from our past—our learned experiences. If we experience the same thing—perhaps having money issues—numerous times, we are strengthening the pathways that create that specific feeling or reaction. In this case, it's the fear and loss of control—the perceived *stress*—that comes from not having enough money. As a matter of fact, we can even become more sensitive to that issue when it does happen. For example, the first time you had money issues, you may not have reacted as strongly as you did the tenth time. Doctors say that severe allergies can actually get worse over time. So every time that you experience an allergic reaction to something, the reaction gets worse than it was the time before. Well, that's true about stress as well. If we condition ourselves to get nervous and upset about something, then the next time such a situation occurs, we'll get even more upset and stressed than we were the previous time. It's important that we recognize that a lot of the stress that we experience arises because we have trained ourselves to think and feel negatively about that particular situation. The good news is that we can reprogram ourselves to create new pathways, avoiding stress.

Smile Action Steps

* Write down one breakdown that you are currently having right now. Make sure you mention only the facts and not your thoughts, feelings, or opinions about it.

_____

_____

_____

_____

_____

_____

* The only way to have a breakthrough with a breakdown is to ask yourself, "What am I committed to in this area of my life?" So now write a statement of what you are committed to having happen with this breakdown—and make sure it's something positive, not, "I am committed to never speaking to that son-of-a-gun again." A more powerful and positive commitment

could be, "I am committed to having a nurturing and powerful relationship with this person."

_____

_____

_____

_____

_____

_____

_____

✳ Ask yourself, what is the learning experience that you can glean from this challenge?

_____

_____

_____

_____

_____

_____

_____

CHAPTER 14

POWERFUL COMMUNICATIONS AT HOME AND AT WORK

*The greatest problem in communication is the illusion
that it has been accomplished.*

—George Bernard Shaw

Any meaningful transformation in your life will naturally involve those who are closest to you. Your key relationships at home and at work—whether they support you or hold you back—will play a major role. Whom you choose to associate with and how you communicate with these people will help to determine the level of success you're able to achieve.

When I was growing up, my mother said something to me that I'll never forget: "Show me your friends and you show me who you are." Naturally, when you say this to an eight-year-old, it's hard for him to comprehend exactly what it means. But now, as an adult, I can see how powerful and full of wisdom that statement is.

Tony Robbins, one of the best motivational and transformational speakers, says that if you were to take your five closest friends and come up with the average income of that group, it probably comes pretty close to your annual income. (I did this exercise myself, and I found that he was correct.) Why is Tony Robbins's statement, along with my mother's, so accurate? It's because the people we hang out and associate with shape our reality.

Have you ever met somebody who always seems to be financially challenged? There's a good chance that this person is constantly complaining about her circumstances. It's the government's fault; it's the social programs; it's her no-good family who won't help her out; or, best yet, she might have conspiracy theories. But none of these alone is the problem.

What creates this person's reality is that she's making these complaints to other people who share the same *stinkin' thinkin'* philosophy. So now you don't have just the one person—you have a group of people, all of whom are complaining about the same issues. And they are all in agreement about the complaints that they're sharing. They might even have regularly scheduled times when they get together to have these conversations. The people in this group are creating a self-perpetuating "bubble" around their lives. What I mean by this is that as humans, we crave to be validated. We want to be right, and we want to have others acknowledge our "correctness" by agreeing with us. So, we're naturally drawn to those who think the way we do. And together, our group insulates us from opinions that conflict with what we believe. Hence, the bubble.

That said, if you're not careful, this can become a vicious cycle, and you can get trapped inside, with these people validating what you think and you validating their thoughts. Likewise, successful people have created a positive bubble to surround themselves with other positive people—and you can (and should) too.

Hanging around with other supportive, positive people will push you beyond your limitations and enable you to have the breakthroughs that you're looking for in life. (This is true, by the way, for folks you associate with in person, the television shows you watch, or any other media or social media that might influence you.) I'll cycle back to negative relationships in just a bit. For now, let's focus on the importance of clear communication in our interactions with others to create positive relationships.

Clear Communication

Communication can be the creator *or* the killer of relationships. That may sound odd, but if you consider all the relationships you've had that didn't go in the direction you wanted them to, it probably was the result of some form of miscommunication and/or misunderstanding. Similarly, if we look at the crises that occur around the world, they typically boil down to something not being communicated or something being misunderstood in some way. Let's look at the ingredients of strong communication between you and the people in your life.

Be Responsible

If you're trying to deliver a message and the receiver—for whatever reason—does not understand or misinterprets your communication, who's responsible? You are! Regardless of how well you think you spoke, if there's a breakdown in the communication process, it's your responsibility. Why? Because ultimately you're the one who's trying to get your message across. By deliberately accepting this ultimate responsibility, and not indulging in anger or blame that the person didn't understand you the first time, you now have the mindset and the power to adjust your technique (change the way you said it, change the medium through which you said it, and so on) in order to make the communication more effective this time.

Listen to the "Listening"

Most of the time, when we communicate, we focus on ourselves and the words we are using to convey our point. If there is a breakdown in communication, what defines the breakdown is not what you said, but whether or not the *other* person understood what you said. Therefore, a more powerful way of thinking is to focus on how the other person is listening to your communication. Try to tailor your message to the other person's *listening*. In other words, be attentive to how someone else might perceive you and what you're saying. The cues that you can pick up from him will help tell you what words you need to use in order for that person to receive your communication.

Set the Context

One of the biggest mistakes you can make is to assume that people know where you're coming from when you start talking. (This issue ties in with respecting and being attuned to their listening.) In almost every situation, it's wise to take a few moments and lay the groundwork for your message *before* you start speaking (or, in a letter or e-mail, at the very beginning of the document). For instance, before you dive in and tell your business prospect all about your wonderful product, first offer the reason for your conversation to begin with—the context, if you will. You'd be amazed at how many folks skip this step. And, it's just common sense.

People care about themselves and their own needs first and foremost. They have automatic thinking already going on, and if you just dive in with your own agenda, you'll literally be speaking to them and the little voice inside their heads will be wondering, "Why is she even telling me this?" You need to take charge and speak to what the person's concerns are. For instance, start by asking your prospect at the very beginning of the meeting to tell you what his biggest challenges are or what his vision is for his department or company over the next 12 months. There are many questions that will draw this out, but being direct works best. "What goal are you trying to reach in your business?" "What's been stopping you from getting there thus far?" "How do you think I might be able to help?" "What in particular can I show you in the time we have together that might be of interest?" Once you have these answers, you can tailor your presentation appropriately. (Now, it's best if you can get these answers on an initial call prior to a face-to-face meeting, but even if you don't and you already have a PowerPoint or other show cued up and ready to go, just knowing these answers will allow you to speak to the listener's concerns when you actually present, as opposed to simply talking about yourself (or being perceived as doing so). This could be the difference between making a sale and going home empty-handed.

Setting the proper context for communication is crucial outside the office as well. And it's equally vital both for major topics and for "the little things." For example, let's say that you intend to sit down and talk with your teenage daughter about the need for her to study more to get her grades up. Before you speak with her, consider what your reason is to want her to do this in the first place. I am going to assume it's because you want her to be able to get into a better college, which, in turn, will help her to achieve more of what she wants in life and to become the successful and independent woman you know she can be. Well, if that's what your motivation is, you need to share that! When you sit down to speak with her, tell her that you love her, respect her, and are looking for ways to make her life even better than it is now. This will create a whole different way of listening in her than if you had just told her that you expect her to study more (which she may interpret as getting scolded by you and respond to with guilt, defiance, or some other emotion that causes you to react, leading to a quick downward spiral into argument).

Be Committed to the Relationship

A key to having effective communication with someone is to be more committed to the relationship than to your opinion or to an effort to prove the other person wrong. What is one of the top reasons why relationships fall apart? Because of a series of arguments. And why do arguments happen? Because we have an opinion that we strongly wish to get across. In any conversation, we're actually more committed to being "right" about our opinion and how we feel than we are about mutual understanding.

When you approach somebody with the sole motive of insisting on your own personal opinion, what are you automatically doing to the other person in the conversation? You're saying that he's wrong. He, in turn, will try to prove you wrong, and the vicious cycle continues to the point where it explodes.

Now, what does this cost us in the process? It costs us the relationship. No opinion is more important than your relationship with the people in your life who mean the most to you. If you can keep this concept in mind while you communicate, your loved one will naturally be more receptive to what you have to say, and together you'll be able to communicate more effectively.

Don't Ask a Question When You Make a Statement

One of the errors we make in communicating with others is that we ask our loved ones a question that is actually a statement in disguise. For example, my fiancée needs a good amount of time to get ready in the morning. Actually, she needs more than two hours. (I am *so* not kidding—ask her yourself!) Anyway, when we have to go somewhere, I naturally give her a warning before we have to leave the house. Now, of course, I think 10 minutes is plenty of time to get ready, but I have learned that this is definitely not the case. As a matter of fact, it probably would be best if I started the warning the night before!

After this happened a few times, April asked me a *question* that sounded like this: "Why do you insist on giving me only 10 minutes' notice to leave the house?" Hmmm. I'm pretty sure that's not really a question. Now, I know that what she truly meant to say was: "Honey, I love you and I want us to have a stress-free life, and I always want to look my best for you and for myself. I would appreciate if you would make it a point to give me more notice in the future (so that I don't kill you—*just kidding!*)."

Kidding aside, when we make a statement that's disguised as a question, (like "Why do you insist on giving me only 10 minutes' notice?"), we're not being straightforward and honest. By asking a question like this, we are actually forcing the other person to justify his actions (which we find annoying), even while we disguise our true feelings with regard to the situation. By forcing the person to defend his position without taking any accountability for our own, we will almost certainly descend into an argument. It's far better to express yourself with integrity and to even make a request (similar to what I interpreted April to really want) rather than play word games. This will avoid future misunderstandings.

Have No Judgments and/or Opinions

To communicate effectively, empty your brain of "already opinions" about how someone is going to react to what you have to say. If you are certain about her response before you even have the conversation, chances are that you are going to behave in a way that will actually trigger the response you are predicting will occur . . . whether you believe that response to be negative or not.

Be Empathetic

It's vital that you show concern and appreciation for the other person's point of view. Actually listen with a clear mind and an open and willing heart. Try to "get" the person's position and absorb where it's coming from. Consider whether there's some way you can help before you respond. This is a subject that tends to be particularly challenging for a lot of men. For the purposes of this chapter on family, let's just say that husbands have been known to struggle with this, as they jump to the "solution-finding" phase before allowing their wives to adequately share their thoughts and emotions about the subject at hand. (Before I get nasty letters, let me acknowledge that the male/female comparison is not an absolute, although it is a tendency. It could possibly be the opposite in your particular relationship.)

Let me give you an example. If your wife comes home and is upset about something that happened with "Jane" at work, let her tell you about the entire situation before you jump 15 steps ahead and tell her the "answer" to how to deal with Jane. And, fellas, while she's telling you, *really listen* to what she is saying. For the sake of your relationship, it's vital that you try to put yourself in her shoes and feel what she feels. That's what empathy is all about.

Be Quick to Say "I'm Sorry"

If you have a communication that turns into an argument, and if you truly are committed to the well-being of the relationship, there is only one thing to say, and that's, "I'm sorry." This is easier said than done, though, because in order to say those two magic words, you have to let go of wanting to be right about winning the argument. "But why should I do that if I truly *was* right?" Here's why: because you're more committed to the relationship than you are to your opinion.

Start Over

There may be times when you just know that nothing productive is going to come out of a conversation *at that moment*. We all have those days when we're just out-and-out cranky or exhausted, or maybe one (or both) of you hasn't eaten since breakfast. It's good to recognize that forcing a conversation under those circumstances is not going to go well. It's OK. The absolute best thing you can do at those times is to say, "Let's start over." Whether it's in 15 minutes or the next morning, believe me, this simple technique works.

The Communication Process

Here are two examples of powerful communication. First, we'll use one from a business situation. Then, we'll look at one that deals with your personal life. The two conversations have the same strategy, but it may help you to see them both in action.

Step 1: Honor Them

What's important to most people is that they be heard and be understood without judgment being passed on them. So, by your approaching them, honoring them for who they are, respecting their opinion, and respecting them as people, you open up powerful lines of communication. Accept them for who they are *and* who they are not, even if you believe they should behave in a different way. Being overly opinionated and judgmental kills off effective communication. Respect and honor the people you are speaking to exactly as they are, and for what they can become.

Step 2: Listen for What They Are Committed To

Many times we enter into a communication focused more on what's important to *us* than on the other person's needs. The reason I call this step "listen for what they are committed to" is that it's not always obvious what people may want from a conversation. They may say one thing, but there's something else that's more important to them. For example, let's say you're an employee at a department store and a customer comes to you because she is very upset about a purchase that she made. She may be complaining and asking for something that's beyond company policy. Now, on the surface, we might think that what the customer is committed to is the thing that she's complaining about. But what she might really want is simply for you to be committed to helping her, serving her, and caring about her upset. So, in this example, all you may need to do is show the customer how much you care about her upset and tell her, "Let me see what I can do to help you. I totally understand and I don't blame you for being upset."

Step 3: Generate Opportunity

This step can have different versions depending on the situation. For example, if you are an employee working for a company, the customer is asking for money back, and that's something that you're not able to do— *and* if the customer's commitment is truly to feel that you care about her upset—there might be an opportunity for you to offer the customer something else that doesn't cost the company money.

Generating opportunity might also mean that you help people stay focused on what's truly important to them, their commitment, rather than their upset. For example, let's say you are a real estate agent in the middle of a negotiation between a buyer and a seller. There is an issue over the refrigerator. The buyers start talking about how they want the refrigerator to stay, and the sellers say that they want the refrigerator themselves and it's not staying, and all of a sudden everybody is seemingly fixated on the refrigerator (this may sound silly, but I've seen it happen!).

Now, the truth is that the sellers are committed to selling and the buyers are committed to buying, but they start to get caught up "in the box" about thoughts, feelings, and opinions, which actually pulls them away from their commitment to buying or selling. In this example, the agent would need to refocus the sellers, perhaps by saying, "Let me ask you, are you committed to a refrigerator, or are you committed to selling your house and moving to Florida?" Or, perhaps with the buyers it would be, "Are you committed to a refrigerator or to creating great memories for your family in this new house?"

An Example of the Communication Process in Divorce

Let's now take a look at using the same process in a personal example. I've chosen divorce as my scenario because my experience has been that people who go through divorces find them to be one of the most dramatic or upsetting experiences in their lives.

Step 1: Honor Them

This step is perhaps the hardest, especially when there is a major upset between you and your ex. However, you must honor your ex as another human being. I mean, at one point you must have had strong positive thoughts and feelings about this person. During a divorce, it's very easy to get away from those feelings. Try to honor your ex for who he used to be for you. That person you once cared about is the same person who you are divorcing, but when you're going through it, you look for all his bad points to justify your new position of winning at something, whether it's winning in material things or winning your opinion. If you let go of the anger you have now and honor him as another human being who you once cared about, you'll be able to get through this divorce with a lot less stress and upset.

Step 2: Listen for What They Are Committed To

I believe that we interpret people's actions based on our opinion of them. If, during a divorce, you believe that your ex is committed to hurting you, to winning a battle, no matter what he does, you will interpret it as a negative action toward you. He could be getting a sip of water from the fountain and you would read that as some sort of plot to bring you down. But let's take your worries and concerns out of the equation and put yourself on the other side of this relationship. What do you think that person is ultimately committed to?

I'm going to suggest that perhaps his commitment could be to move on with his life—to create a new chapter where he can be happy in a relationship. If, underneath all the arguments and upsets and name-calling, you can tune into *that* commitment and focus on that desire to live happily and fully, you might have a new appreciation for him, and he for you.

You'll notice that this changes a little bit when children are involved. During divorce, parents have no right to be concerned solely about themselves. Their number one priority is to be committed to their children and make sure that the children come out of this unscathed.

Now let's assume two possible scenarios. One scenario is that your ex cares about, and is committed to, your children as much as you are, but that he has lost sight of that commitment because of that "winning at any cost" mentality that occurs in a divorce. If this is the case, by your simply bringing back to the surface that "we've got to make decisions and have conversations that are in the best interests of our children," you can actually have a productive conversation. The other possible scenario is that your ex does not have the same understanding and appreciation of how much trauma children go through during divorce, and therefore may not be open to any thoughts or suggestions that you might have that are in the best interests of the children. If your ex cares more about himself than about the well-being of your child or children, then you should take whatever action is necessary to protect their well-being. I'm not talking about custody here; I'm talking about emotional well-being. I can best communicate this point with you by sharing a personal story.

When my relationship with my son's mother ended, we both agreed that it would be best for my son if I had residential custody. There were many reasons for this arrangement, but one of the major ones was that my son considered our house to be his home, and my ex did not want to have my son go through the trauma of not living in his home. That is one example where my ex was more committed to my son's well-being than what she may have actually wanted. Kudos to her. But that's not the main example I want to share. There was one incident where my son's mother was aggravating me, and in passing, I happened to share with my son what was going on, and I was not saying the most complimentary things about his mother. It wasn't too bad, but I was complaining about his mother. Michael was 15 at the time. After I left his room, I went back in there five minutes later and said to him, "Don't you dare ever let anybody say anything negative about your mother, including me. What I did was a mistake. Any challenges between your mother and me have nothing to do with who she is with you and your relationship with her. She is your mother, so you should always love her, respect her, and stand up for her no matter what." I knew it was crucial for my son to have a strong, nurturing, loving relationship with his mother. I had to sacrifice my own opinions for his well-being, and every child needs to have a good relationship with both his parents. The child should not be in therapy as an adult because the parents couldn't be in a relationship with each other anymore.

Step 3: Generate Opportunity

If everybody in a divorce has the same commitments toward their mental well-being and having their life move forward, then a tremendous number of opportunities exist. You can become friends and can support each other. When you have had a life together for many years, it's a shame to throw it all away because of a divorce. This is usually what happens when people get too wrapped up in being right about their thoughts, feelings, and opinions. When it comes to the children, it's even more important that there be some opportunity for everybody to be in some form of relationship that isn't based on anger and upset.

I'll continue with my personal story to help illustrate this point. As of the writing of this book, I found the love of my life—I would say my soul mate—two years ago, and her name is April. She and my son get along tremendously, and I love her, so we've got a whole family. To quote Michael, "Unlike a lot of my friends who have gone through divorces where somebody doesn't like somebody, I'm lucky because I've got two families." Now, my ex has since married, and she and her husband were recently looking to buy a house. They decided to contact my fiancée, who happens to be a real estate agent. So imagine this: my fiancée is taking my ex and her husband, showing them properties to help them find their new home. This opportunity for everybody to get along so wonderfully exists for the sake of my son. Everyone involved is committed to making a positive environment for him that isn't based on anger and resentment.

Communicating with Our Children

As you can tell by my examples throughout this book, and especially in the last section, I believe that our families are hugely important in our lives. And nothing is more important than our relationship with our children. Now, this is such an important section of the book that I'm not sure I can fully do it justice. In fact, this topic deserves its own book! The bottom line is, I believe that when it comes to children, as parents or grand-parents, our job is very simple: to lay a powerful foundation for them so that they can grow to be healthy, happy adults. Their ability to do so also affects us as parents or grandparents and increases the joy in our lives.

Although we cannot control every experience that our children have, we want to do our best to influence them as much as we possibly can as they start to learn about relationships, love, friendship, business, and other such things. Toward that end, I have two simple areas that I focus on when it comes to raising my son: (1) creating memorable moments and (2) teaching him life lessons.

Memorable Moments

I want you to think back to your childhood. If I were to ask you to share with me anything that you remember about growing up, you probably would start to tell me about a moment, an experience. You probably still retain vivid details of some of the most memorable times. We can almost say that our life is just a string of these moments, and that these moments have influenced you so much that they have helped to shape and create the person you are today. By purposely setting out to create memorable moments for your child, you can help shape how your child is going to grow up as an adult. I can think of nothing more import-ant than actively participating in your child's life, and having special moments that you share (and which your child will remember) is a way to deepen your communication and enhance your bond.

To give you a sense of what I'm talking about, let me rattle off just a few of the memorable moments that I created with my son.

When Michael was very young, I took him on a skiing trip with his friends. This was "the boys event," and we did it for one weekend each winter no matter what. It was during this time that "the boys" would bond and share moments. I would discuss certain life lessons with them, such as planning their time, being responsible for packing their gear, and having fun while respecting others. This was a time that my son and his friends will probably remember into their adulthood.

To me, the best place to celebrate the Fourth of July is in Washington, DC. When Michael was young, during our first trip to the capital, he got to see the fireworks; go to some of the national historic sites such as Ford's Theatre, the Washington Monument, the Lincoln Memorial, and the Library of Congress (where you can actually see a copy of one of my books); and, of course, take a White House tour. This trip, for me, was about opening his eyes to his heritage as an American, showing him the wonder of what some of the great men before him had accomplished and, hopefully, instilling in him a love of history and the desire to learn more academically.

When my son entered high school in the ninth grade, I wanted him to have a vision of what he was working toward. So I called Notre Dame University and arranged a tour to show my son what college life at a very reputable university would be like. This trip is a perfect example of influencing our children to enable them to see their futures. After that trip, Michael wanted to deck out his bedroom with all Notre Dame paraphernalia. So now, during his high school years, he recognizes that the end result is really to get into a good university so that he can get the best education possible. Now, honestly, at the time we took this tour, I wasn't financially capable of paying the tuition that a university like Notre Dame would require. But I have a firm belief that when you make a commitment, the circumstances will eventually fall in line behind that commitment. Touring Notre Dame was not about my son choosing Notre Dame, it was about him having a vision of what was possible in his future when he completed high school. By the way, every year since he began high school, I've taken him to other colleges so that we can continue to envision his future possibilities.

You may think that in order to create a memorable moment for your child, you have to spend a lot of money or go on trips or vacations. However, there are many other smaller activities that you can do that will help influence the type of person your child will become as an adult. Here are just a few examples of those memorable moments that you can make with your child:

* Easter egg hunts
* Singing a song together
* Making dinner together

* Going window shopping during the holidays when the stores first decorate their windows
* Going to the lake
* Fishing
* Playing board games
* Playing video games
* Going on ordinary errands (to the supermarket or gas station), but making it an adventure for your children

Even though these are "minor" actions, as opposed to trips across the country, for example, they each demonstrate a few things. First, and without a doubt, they show our children that we love them and that we want to spend time with them, even when it's just the day-to-day stuff like making dinner or going shopping. Second, each time we spend these moments with our children, we have an opportunity to communicate. We don't always have to talk about something profound, but we can certainly ask questions, take an interest in their lives (about what they are learning, who their friends are, where they see themselves in a few years, and so on—with different questions appropriate for different ages, of course). The bottom line is that children need to know that they can count on you no matter what, and they will remember your being there for them, which in turn means that they'll be more open with you, and as a result, you'll have more and more opportunities to help shape their lives in a positive direction.

The thing that really works about these memorable moments is when they start to become a family tradition. It is in doing the same activity on a regular basis that real memories get created. As a side note, be prepared for some of these traditions to eventually drop off. For example, when my son was 16, we didn't go skiing or go to Washington, DC, for the Fourth of July. Honestly, I was a little sad about that, but my son was getting to an age where that memory was not important to him anymore. But I do know that when he's in his late twenties or thirties and he starts having his own children, he'll remember those moments and perhaps hand them down and help put a smile on the face of his children.

The second area I want to discuss with you is teaching your child life lessons. These are not the memorable moments that you purposely create with them. These are simply what happens to them as they experience various aspects of life. And it is very important that you be there for them during these times, because when your child is exposed to something for the *first time*, he's going to create a "rule" about life that will influence his decisions from then on. That's right, this is the beginning of the formation of what will become his automatic thinking. For example, when a teenager falls in love for the first time, that experience is going to create that teenager's rules about love. The first time a child plays a game, whether it's a board game or a physical game, if she loses that game, how she handles that loss is going to dictate how she handles losses in her life as an adult. It's during these times, those first moments, that it's very important that we as parents guide our children. Since you have the benefit of some self-knowledge and introspection that you've gained from reading this book, you are aware that humans don't have to become trapped by their automatic thoughts—that we are free to create and live "outside the box" that we might otherwise build around ourselves.

Here is a partial list of some of the "first moments" for our children that I think we need to provide life lessons for:

* They feel rejected by another child.
* An adult seems to be unfair to them.
* They get a failing grade on a test.
* They fail at a project or game.
* They have their first romantic relationship.
* They have their first breakup (this is a biggie).
* They have a fight with a best friend.
* They go to their first unsupervised party.
* They go to a new school.
* They try out for a sport.
* They fail to make a sports team or a club.
* They try out for a play.
* They learn an instrument and play in a concert.

You need to help guide your children during each of these events and teach them to be responsible for their own actions and for how they treat others, to play full out, to get back up after they've fallen down, and to value themselves, knowing that no one else has a say in their own self-worth. Of course, each "first moment" calls for a slightly different lesson, but the important thing is that you are there, you are listening, and you are taking an active role in helping your children become healthy, happy adults with plenty of reasons to smile!

Smile Action Steps

 If you have any negative relationships in your life that are robbing you of joy, what can you do to create a positive bubble around yourself so that you don't let that negativity infect you?

_____

_____

_____

_____

_____

_____

_____

 If you are having a tough time with someone important in your life, what can you do to make improvements in that relationship?

_____

_____

_____

_____

_____

_____

_____

❋ What are some "memorable moments" that you can create with your family (children, grandchildren, or even parents)?

_____

_____

_____

_____

_____

_____

_____

❋ If you have a child or grandchild and you are concerned about his emotional well-being, take the time to have a conversation with him to make sure he is OK.

CREATE A POSITIVE WORK ENVIRONMENT AND LOVE YOUR JOB

*A man at work, making something which he feels will exist
because he is working at it and wills it, is exercising the energies
of his mind and soul as well as his body.*

—William Morris

I n this chapter, I want to tell you why smiling is so important in any profession or job, and also give you some strategies for creating a career worth smiling about.

As you've seen throughout this book, smiling can have a positive impact on every area of your life. And the "smile cycle"—smiling more helps us get what we want, and, in turn, getting what we want helps us to smile more, setting up a wonderful, self-reinforcing pattern—is alive and well in the workplace. Smiling in your job is therefore vitally important. The majority of people dedicate more daily hours to their work than to any other pursuit, including family, leisure, household activities, and even sleeping. With this much time invested, don't you want your career to be something that makes you happy?

For Business Owners and Managers

If you're a business owner or manager, smiling is one of the most important leadership skills that you should develop. And I don't believe that's an overstatement. Part of being a good leader is helping your team to be as productive as possible and create a positive impact on the bottom line. Studies show that a happy team member is a productive team member. Smiling makes staff members feel good, which also increases their attention and creativity. When this idea was tested in 2010, the results showed that participants who smiled performed better on cognitive tasks that required "seeing the whole forest, rather than just the trees."[1] So a smile really can help give us a burst of insight.

There are many skill sets that a leader needs to have, but two stand out for me. The first is to *have a clear vision* for your team and/or your company, and the second is to *get your team inspired* about that vision. After all, the more those on your team believe in your vision, the harder they will work to make that vision a reality. Now, smiling is a vital skill that will help you to articulate that vision and to get your team 100 percent behind you. By communicating your vision with passion, and by displaying a trusting and approachable manner, you'll find that people will gravitate to you and will more easily support what you have to say.

Here's another thing. People don't like working for those who they don't like, and it's really hard to like a sourpuss. So, if you want to have a happy, productive team that is inspired by your vision, you must communicate each message with a smile.

Job Interviews for the Employee

Having a nice appearance at job interviews goes beyond the suit or blazer that you're wearing. Whatever clothes you're wearing, it's imperative that you top them off with a terrific smile. Researchers conducted a study that asked participants to look at full-length photographs of 123 people and then describe what personality traits these strangers might possess, based on how they looked.[2] The people in the photos either (1) were genuinely smiling or (2) wore a neutral expression. The smiling people were assigned traits such as "likable, confident, conscientious, and stable." These are obviously traits that someone would be looking for in an employee, so make sure that a smile is part of what you put on that morning.

Here's another kind-of-obvious fact, even if it sounds politically incorrect to acknowledge it. Study after study indicates that people who are considered "attractive" are given more opportunities to be hired and subsequently to advance in their jobs than those who are not thought of in this light. And, smiling, as we've well documented, makes people more appealing to others. So, make sure you bring that smile along when you sit down to discuss your job!

For the Salesperson

I'm not just talking about people who have a traditional "product" to sell. Regardless of what profession you're in, chances are that you will have to be a salesperson at one time or another. For instance, a dentist may have to sell a nervous patient on the idea of a particular procedure, a store owner may sell to potential customers by providing great service, and even a politician has to sell his ideas to voters and fellow politicians.

No matter what you are selling, whether it's an idea, a service, or a product, when you smile, you project a more welcoming, warmer tone to those who are listening. It will even help you in increasing your sales.

An interesting study done at Bangor University in Wales found that individuals were even willing to pay more when they were dealing with those whom they considered to be genuinely smiling.[3] The research involved asking students to play a game against computerized opponents in which they could win money. The opponents were represented by avatars that smiled either *genuinely* or *mildly* (aka *politely*). As they played, students came to understand that certain opponents gave them a better chance to win. Participants were then asked to choose which opponents they preferred to play against during each round.

The researchers had expected the students to value winning money above all else. However, they found that students chose the *genuinely* smiling opponents first, even when those opponents gave them less of a chance to win.

Since we're all in sales in one way or another, remember to keep that smile on your face and show that you genuinely love what you do and that you love serving others. It's sure to pay off!

Ideas to Create a Work Environment to Smile About

Here are a slew of ideas for things you can do to help create a work environment that's worth smiling about.

You Make a Difference

Let me ask you a question. When you are on the customer side of things, how do you like to be treated? Let's say you call the phone company to check on a concern that you have about your plan or your service. And let's say that you speak to someone who you can tell is having a bad day, and who is not really committed to helping you. You can tell she is just waiting for 5:00 p.m. to come. How does that make you feel? More important, how does it make you feel about the company as a whole? That person who answered the phone can help make or break the relationship between the company and the customer. And even if your position does not directly interact with the customer, you still make a difference. If you took everyone in your department out of the company and dissolved that department, I suspect the company would have a tough time functioning. So you and everyone in your department make a difference to the whole.

Be Committed to Mastering Your Job Skill

What would make you happier? To work at a job where you feel you have a higher purpose to improve the world around you, or to simply work for a paycheck? (I hope the answer is obvious.) It's very easy to get caught up in the cycle of going to your job and simply doing the same things over and over again. You know, "same old, same old." When this starts to happen and the excitement and joy of the job wear off, what's left is that it's just something you're doing to get a paycheck. But it will create more joy in your job, and therefore keep putting a smile on your face, if you make a commitment to improving your skill at your job. If you can stay committed to mastering your job, it'll be much more interesting. This is similar to being a black belt in the martial arts. As I mentioned in Chapter 8, those who are black belts will tell you that being a black belt is not a destination, but rather a way of living. When you are committed to mastery, you're constantly looking to improve your skill. Therefore, it's not a destination, but a place to live from. I suggest that you become a black belt at your job.

When you master your job, it becomes much more fun and exciting. When I do my live seminars, I'll usually ask the audience, "How many of you are bakers?," and usually a small percentage of hands will be raised. I then say to the group, "You should all be raising your hands because at some level, you are all bakers. If you wanted to bake a cake, you could simply go down to the supermarket, buy a box of cake mix, mix it with the other ingredients following all the directions, and voilà, you baked a cake." So everybody in my audience is a baker, but the chefs are the ones who can bake a cake from scratch. As a matter of fact, master chefs can actually create their own recipes. Now someone who has a job, gets a paycheck, and is committed only to the paycheck is the premade cake baker. But the person who is really skilled at his or her job is the chef. And when you become so skilled at your profession that you become a chef, you will be much more successful.

Be Valuable

When you are committed to improving your job skills, you also become more valuable to your employer. Any business owner will tell you that it costs more money to hire a new person and train him or her than it does to keep an employee who is already skilled at his or her job and effective. So the more skilled you become, and the more productive you are, the more secure your job is. Find out what your workplace really needs in order to become successful, and commit yourself to providing that function. It might be a particular computer skill, advanced research, a new way to create proposals, or marketing ideas. Constantly surprise those around you—whether you are in charge or an employee—with your commitment to do what it takes to advance the cause of your organization.

No Drama in the Workplace

I don't know of any office that doesn't have some kind of drama or personality challenges between people. It's important that you not get caught up in that drama. All that will do is drain you, and even weaken your job security. Enjoy your colleagues, be nice and courteous, but remember, the company has a higher purpose—and that's the customer. If there are no customers, there's no company. If there is no company, there's no job.

Be Committed to Helping Others at Work

Become known as the "go-to" person who is willing to give a helping hand to a colleague. Just as you have a Next Level that you want to reach, each of your colleagues has goals as well. Find out what they really want to achieve and what you can do to help them get there.

Focus on the Customer

I know what you're thinking: "I hope Darryl's not going to say that the customer is always right." I'm not, because it's not about right or wrong.

But I will say this: if your company had no customers, there would be no company. And if there were no company, you would have no job. Every time a customer gives the company money for something, a piece of that money goes to you. It might be a small percentage, but you definitely get a "piece of the action," as we say in New York. So the happier your customers are, the more money they spend, which means conceptually that the better off you are. Even if you are on a fixed salary, you get a piece of that money in two ways: more job security and the possibility of better raises and/or advancement. Take care of the customers, and you take care of your future.

Manage Your Time Wisely

There are countless books, seminars, and courses devoted to time management. The reason for this heavy interest is that many of us become distracted quite easily and can use all the help we can get in managing our time (especially in today's hectic world, where social media, 24-hour cable news channels, and video games bombard our senses all day long). When you're at your job, though, there are a few things that you can do to help you boost your efficiency.

Do What You *Don't* Like First

This is almost counterintuitive, right? Why should you purposely look to do things that you dislike? Because by getting the things that you would typically avoid out of the way early in the day or week, you remove a large weight from your shoulders—even if it was just subconscious—and this will free you up to be that much more creative and effective moving forward. In addition, as we said earlier, we have only a certain amount of willpower, so if you deplete it doing other activities, when it comes time to do the thing you dislike the most, you may find that you don't have enough willpower to tackle it.

Recognize What's Urgent Versus What's Important

We all have lots of urgent things to deal with each day. There are random phone calls, e-mails, guests or coworkers who knock on our door, or even unexpected problems such as deadlines that change without notice or clients who need immediate assistance. There will be tasks that must be attended to right away, but don't lose sight of the need to work on the things that are important. Important items are those that will truly get us to our Next Level, but that will never happen on their own unless we proactively plan to do them. These are items like taking a course to get a degree that will help you climb the ladder at work, or spending quality time with your family. Don't compromise and let the items that are urgent prevent us from doing the things that are important. Schedule some time each day (put it on your calendar!) to do the things that are important, and make sure that you don't let urgent things get in the way.

Learn to Say No

There's no more powerful word in the time management universe than these two simple letters: N O. You cannot possibly tackle everything and be involved in every aspect of an office. So, if you are asked to take on more than you can possibly handle, know when you can politely decline, and take advantage of that option.

Box Yourself In

"Boxing yourself in" has also been referred to as "throwing your hat over the wall." This means deliberately doing something that gives you no option but to go forward. There's no turning back! For me, this would include training for the marathon, as I described earlier in the book. Something I did to literally give myself no choice but to train was to get dropped off at four in the morning 10 miles away from my home. I kind of had to start running at that point, right? Similarly, when I chose to improve my health by losing weight, one of the first things I did was to make the commitment "live" in front of one of my training classes, complete with the number of pounds I was going to lose and the deadline to achieve my goal. With so many people now aware of my commitment, I couldn't let them all down without suffering a great deal of embarrassment. Look for opportunities where you can commit to reaching your Next Level at work in such a way that you "have no choice" but to succeed.

Schedule Your Life

One of your challenges may be to better balance your time amongst family, your business, and whatever may be left over for yourself. If you don't take care of all these areas, you will find that you don't have a life worth smiling about. So here are some suggestions to that end:

* First, understand that you have only 168 hours each week, so you have to decide how many of those 168 hours are going to go to each of those three areas of your life.
* Schedule the actual time on the actual day of the week when you are going to focus on one of the three categories. For example, let's say you reserve 30 hours a week for yourself. You may decide that you are going to work out or read from 6:00 a.m. to 8:00 a.m. Monday, Wednesday, and Friday—you just scheduled 6 of your 30 hours.
* Leave your personal life at home and leave your work at your work. I know this is hard to do sometimes, but it's important that when you are at work, you are able to focus on your job. If you must attend to some personal items during the day, make sure you limit it to a designated time—maybe while you're at lunch or on break.
* From time to time, you may feel like you are always either starting a "to-do" item, finishing a "to-do" item, or in the middle of a "to-do" item. You are rushing around and trying to accomplish as much as you can, but at the end of the day, you still feel that you haven't accomplished much. Here's something that will help. Break up your to-do list into three categories: what you *must* accomplish, what you *should* accomplish, and what you *could* accomplish this week. Then work the list in that order, starting with the *must* items. I promise that you will have a better sense of accomplishment.

Highlight Your Accomplishments

Lastly, let me tell you a simple way to motivate yourself. When you have a "to-do" list of items that you must accomplish, print it out and place it in front of you. Once you have completed an item, cross it off with a bright yellow highlighter. Sounds old school, right? Especially with all the time management apps for your phone and other systems available, why use this method? Because there's something about seeing your accomplishment highlighted in the brightest possible way that will motivate you and inspire you to get more highlights. I've found that this method is far more effective than a simple checkmark or crossing out an item. Mentally, it creates more of a positive, rewarding feeling. You've heard the expression "success produces more success." Well, accomplishment produces more accomplishments. When you cross *off* items your to-do list, all that's left to focus on at the end of the day are the things that are still there. This is disappointing and not rewarding at all. If instead you highlight what you accomplished, the focus is more on what you *did* do rather than what you *didn't* do. Give it a try and see for yourself!

Smile Action Steps

* What skill can you commit to learning that will make you indispensible at work?

_____

_____

_____

_____

_____

_____

* Name a colleague you can help to achieve his or her Next Level and write down specifically how you can help.

_____

_____

_____

_____

_____

_____

_____

* What item have you been avoiding that if you accomplish it, you will free yourself up to advance in your job?

_____

_____

_____

_____

_____

_____

* How can you "box yourself in"? What commitment will you make to your colleagues or management that will literally put you "out there" and stretch you to reach your Next Level—with no possibility of backing down?

_____

_____

_____

_____

_____

_____

CHAPTER 16

REVERSE POLARITY: TURNING NEGATIVE PEOPLE INTO POSITIVES

When elephants fight, it is the grass that suffers.

—African proverb

As we said earlier, part of designing a life worth smiling about is surrounding yourself with nurturing and supportive people. If you hang around negative people who are always complaining about their circumstances, eventually that will become your reality. This idea goes beyond just the people you associate with.

If you look at your external world, if you're surrounded by positivity and support, your life looks totally different from the way it looks if you are surrounded by negativity. Here's a simplistic example of how your environment can influence you. I've been focused on applying the principles of this book in my personal life. One of the projects that I took on was losing weight and getting healthier. Well, one day my aunt bought my uncle a birthday cake—which sat prominently on the kitchen counter. That delectable cake kept calling my name. Every time I walked past that counter, right there staring me in the face was this wonderful, rich, sweet birthday cake. So what do you think I did? *Noooo*, I didn't eat it until it was all gone. But believe me, the temptation was there. So to keep honoring my commitment (rather than falling into my longstanding habits), I asked my family if they could move the cake somewhere out of my line of sight. (Otherwise I *was* going to eat it all up!)

Along these lines, let me share with you a brief parable related to how each person brings her own perspective to every aspect of life. As you read this, consider which driver you'd rather hang out with and which one will have a better quality of life.

A man pulled into a gas station and asked the attendant, "What are the people like in the next town up ahead?" The attendant said, "What were the people like in the town you just came from?" "They were awful people," the man responded. "Rude, cold, hostile, abrupt, and unfriendly. They wouldn't give me the time of day." "Well," said the attendant, "I'm sorry to say it, but you're going to find exactly the same sort of people in the next town up ahead." A bit later, another driver pulled in, coming from the same direction as the first. "What are the people like in the next town up ahead?" the second man asked. The attendant said, "What were the people like in the town you just came from?" "Wonderful people," the second man responded. "Friendly, warm, helpful, patient, and kind. They went out of their way to help a stranger." "Well," said the attendant, "I'm happy to tell you that you're going to find exactly the same kind of people in the next town up ahead."

So, the drivers had a different interpretation of the same exact thing—one saw the world through a negative lens, and the other had a positive mindset. Which type of person would you rather surround yourself with? Which type is most likely to support you in reaching your goals? It's kind of obvious, right?

Counteracting Negativity

Now, having said all this, despite your best intentions, it's not very likely that you're *only* going to encounter the most optimistic folks on the planet. You need to know how to deal effectively with those who have a disposition that's more sour than your own.

Who's the Negative One?

Determine whether the person is truly negative, or whether it is just that you have a negative opinion about him. I know that might be a strong statement, but this is something you have to make sure of. The truth is, the way we perceive people is based on the judgment and opinions we have about them. You have a lot of power as to how you interpret those around you. Most of the time, what somebody is actually doing or saying isn't what really annoys us. What annoys us is our *opinion* of their behavior. So, check your attitude and be honest with yourself. Is the other person really the problem . . . or is it you?

Think 100 Percent–0 Percent

You've probably heard the expression that relationships are 50-50. But have you ever noticed that whenever a relationship is not working, it's always the other person's 50 percent that's to blame? I learned a long time ago that a more powerful approach to any relationship is to consider it 100 percent–0 percent, meaning that I take 100 percent responsibility for how the relationship looks, and the other person's responsibility is 0 percent. Now, I must admit that this is not always easy for me to do because as a human being, I have a tendency to shift the blame to others, but I also know that when you take 100 percent responsibility for how that relationship looks, you now have the power to influence how that relationship occurs for you.

Be Committed to Putting Smiles on Their Faces

The best way to deal with somebody who's in a negative or nasty mood is to help lift her out of that mood—and the best way to do that is by giving her a smile. Remember the old expression that "you attract more bees with honey"? Let me share a personal story that illustrates this.

A few years ago, I had the opportunity to speak at a national convention in Florida. As is common at many conventions, the sponsoring organization negotiated special pricing at a local attraction. Of course, since the convention was in Orlando, it was for Disney World. The special offer was the Twilight ticket, where you could enter the park after 4 p.m. for about 40 percent of the regular price. Pretty awesome deal! So, my fiancée and I went over to the park and headed to the ticket gate for our twilight tickets. Now, the woman at Disney World had just finished with a *guest* (as Disney calls customers) who was on line ahead of us, and who had not been very nice, to say the least. So, this Disney *cast member* (its name for customer service reps) was visibly not in the best mood as I approached her. I asked to purchase a twilight ticket, and she explained to me that she couldn't sell me the ticket because it had to be purchased directly from the association that was running the convention. Based on where the convention was being held, it would've taken us a good 90 minutes to go back and forth to get this ticket. So, obviously I was very disappointed. But my fiancée and I decided to joke around with the cast member for a bit, to show that we were good sports.

We started saying things like, "Oh, please, isn't there anything you can do? We love Tinker Bell. Don't you have some magical pixie dust behind the counter? You could create a magical moment for me!" And so on. No matter what we tried and no matter how playful we were (smiling the whole time), however, nothing seemed to work. So, the final thing I said to this woman was, "I totally understand, but thank you so much for trying to help us." I said it very sincerely, not sarcastically, and began to leave. I must have been about 10 feet away when all of a sudden I heard a shout from behind me. This cast woman was yelling, "Excuse me, sir! Please come back here." So, I turned back around, and the next thing she did was ask where I was from. I told her I was from New York. She then asked to see my ID. Of course, when you ask a New Yorker for his ID, the next natural response is, "Why? Am I in trouble?" After a few clicks on her keyboard, however, she handed me an envelope with a smile. I opened up the envelope, and what did I see but two free tickets! And not just any free tickets! They were Hopper tickets—which meant that we could go to any one of the parks that we chose—and she didn't even charge me! I felt as if she had just handed me the last Willy Wonka Golden ticket!

Now, while I had been smiling and talking about Tinker Bell and pixie dust, the other guest at the ticket booth next to me was still yelling at the Disney cast member about her inability to get into the park with the ticket she had. I can't tell you all the details because I'm not a skilled eavesdropper, but the bottom line was that she wasn't being allowed into the park. So, while the person next to me was playing the part of Grumpy, my fiancée and I were feeling like Snow White and Happy. We got into the park while that woman was still out at the ticket counter yelling at the poor cast member.

Appreciating and Respecting Others

If somebody is in a bad state of mind and his mood is seeping out onto you, what he might really need is a little bit of love and appreciation. He needs your help to put a smile on his face. And if you can help turn a person's attitude around because of your unselfishness, you will be rewarded.

When someone seems to be negative toward us, we might normally take it personally, and our automatic thinking might say something like, "He's just a jerk!" This kind of involuntary, preprogrammed judgment will only get us angry, rob us of our own joy, and take away our peace. We have the power to make a judgment that is more productive and more nurturing to our own soul. For example, if somebody seems to be coming across as negative, perhaps your judgment can be, "She must be having a bad day," or even something like, "She might have some insecurity issues," or, "This might be a cry for help." Try substituting those thoughts for "She's a jerk!" or something similar. Always assume the best.

You can go even deeper with this idea by saying something to yourself such as, "I need to get to know this person better." If we can assume that every person we encounter has something good within him, there will be more opportunities for us to have healthy and nurturing relationships. Sometimes we may have to dig really deep to find that good because that person has covered it up with so many protective devices, but it's still there. If we approach every person, even the ones whom we have challenges with, with an attitude of respect and of honoring them for the difference that they make in the world, it'll be a lot easier to deal with the negative attitude that they may be displaying at the time. Everyone has some value, everyone has something to contribute, and the more we remember that, the more patient we can be.

Here is a brief story that helps illustrate the concept that everyone has value.

A scientific convention was held at a lakeside resort. After the first day's proceedings, a mathematician, a physicist, an astronomer, and a molecular biologist hired a boatman to row them around on the lake. As they sat in the boat, they discussed string theory, bubble universes, the Gaia hypothesis, and other complex topics. The biologist noticed the boatman looking at them out of the corner of his eyes. He asked him, "What do you think of these ideas?" The boatman replied, "I didn't understand any of it." The astronomer asked him how far he had studied. The boatman told them that he couldn't even read. "I hate to say it," said the physicist, "but you seem to have wasted a good part of your life." The boatman remained silent. By now, they were out in the middle of the lake, far from shore. A sudden storm whipped up. The waves started churning and heaving. All of a sudden, the boat flipped over. The boatman started swimming for shore. The scientists cried out, "Help! We can't swim!" The boatman called back, "I hate to say it, but you seem to have wasted your whole lives."

The four scientists were arrogant and dismissive. Had they tried to be receptive to those around them, such as the boatman, the outcome would have been different. The bottom line: appreciate everyone and his or her contribution to the world.

What if the Person Is Truly Negative?

The premise for this next section may seem to contradict what I just said, but I do believe that there are some people in this world who, no matter what you do or say, you'll still see no possibility of looking at as anything other than negative human beings, or poisons in your life. So, if you have such a person in your life, here are a few suggestions.

Wish People Well

The more you hang onto negative feelings about a person (anger, hatred, disdain, jealousy, disgust, and the like), the more this eats away at you. It's like digesting a poison. So my suggestion here is simply to be happy for those people. Mentally wish them well—and mean it! Happy thoughts create happy feelings, and negative thoughts create negative feelings. You need to smile and be happy, so send out that vibe to others, even the most negative folks you encounter.

Be the Thermostat, not a Thermometer

This concept also applies for situations beyond dealing with negative people. At any moment, we have the power to choose whether we'll be a thermostat or a thermometer. A thermometer is a reactive device that tells you the temperature of the room that it's in. The thermometer reading goes up and down based on what's happening externally to itself. Contrast this with a thermostat, which actually controls the environment. The thermostat tells the environment how we want it to be, hotter or colder. So, we have the choice of being either a thermostat or a thermometer. If we are a thermometer, we're going to be directly influenced by what's happening outside of us. Thus, we'll be at the mercy of what a negative person is doing. But if we behave like a thermostat, not only will this other person not affect us, but we will become a standard for how he should interact with us. In other words, as a thermostat you will set the temperature for how that person should behave when he is around you.

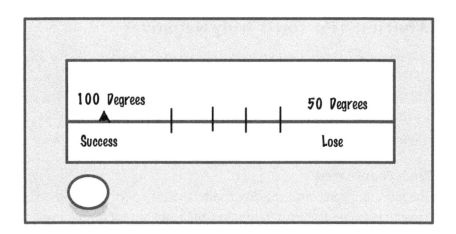

Don't Interact with Those Who Are Truly Negative

The worst thing you can do is argue or engage with a negative person on her terms. There's an old southern saying, "When you wrestle with a pig, you both get dirty." So the best thing for you to do is to stay away from negative people as much as possible to avoid engaging with the bad attitudes that they exude. Try this little exercise with me right now. Take both your hands, open them up, and then bring them together. We call this little gesture "clapping." (Perhaps you've heard of it.) If you do this repeatedly and with others, you will make so much noise that we might call it "applause." Now, take only one hand and swing it in the air as if you are going to clap, but keep your other hand at your side. What happens? There is no noise. You see, it takes two hands to clap and two people to create an argument. The best thing to do is not interact with negative folks when they are being poisonous—the noise eventually goes away.

Remove the Knots

A good friend of mine, Suzanne Greenblatt, told me a story about her daughter's hair. Her daughter has very thick and curly hair, so the sheer process of combing her hair could be a painful challenge, filled with a lot of complaints from the little girl. One day, Suzanne said something to her daughter that was very profound: "Honey, you have to go through the pain of getting these knots out because after that, you're going to have smooth and silky hair." Now, take that one step further.

There are always going to be times in our lives where we have knots to work out in our businesses, our personal lives, and our relationships. Working out these knots can be somewhat painful, but once you go through that short-term pain, you too can have a smooth and silky life.

When a knot is too close to you or too big to work out, the remaining option is to cut it out. Think of the negative "knot" in your life that is dragging you down. Now, when you cut out this knot, you are going to go through some pain. And at the end of it, you'll even have an empty spot that's close to the skin. But after a while, you'll have new hair filling that void. And, most important, you will not have the knot in your life anymore.

Moving Onward and Upward

When you start to grow, some of the people closest to you may want to keep you down. As you start to stretch yourself and do things that make you uncomfortable so that you can attain your Next Level in life, the people who are closest to you are forced to look at their own lives. They then wonder if they are able to move upward as well, to live an extraordinary life. If a person is not ready to look at that question for himself, he might resent you for making him feel uncomfortable—or even inferior. Even though this is not your intention, it is what might be occurring. Also, sometimes the people who are closest to you are afraid that if you grow as a human being, you may grow away from them.

It's important that you be patient and understanding of people in this frame of mind. Reassure them that you love them just the way they are and that there's nothing they need to do to change their lives. Reassure them that you're always going to love them and that you won't grow away from them as you strive to grow and improve your own life.

Change It, Live with It, or Leave It

Let me end this chapter with a concept that I always keep in mind for myself. If you have a really negative person (or situation, for that matter) who is detracting from your life and preventing you from smiling on a regular basis, you really have only three choices of what to do: *either change it, live with it, or leave it.* Anything that is not one of these three choices just perpetuates the negative situation and keeps it alive.

Change it. Yep, this is a great solution. Just change the person. Fix her. Perhaps even try shock therapy. I know, you're thinking, "Darryl, if they would just read *this* book, then my life would be so much better." Actually, when I say, "change it," I'm not talking about changing the other person; rather, I'm talking about changing yourself. You see, we really can't change somebody as much as we would like to think we can. Of all the three options, I find that this is the most doable and most powerful option. We should always look internally and see what actions we can take to improve the situation.

Live with it. Be careful here. By "live with it," I don't mean becoming resigned. I don't mean that you should throw your hands up in the air and say, "There's nothing I can do about it. I have no control at all, so all I can do is just live with it." Obviously, that would not be creating a life worth smiling about. As a matter of fact, that probably would create a life worth being miserable about. I am talking here about peaceful acceptance. This is a shift that comes internally. You are purposely changing your thoughts, feelings, or judgments concerning how your life (with regard to this person or situation) should look or be different. Put simply, you have no more expectations that the person or situation will change, and you are truly OK with things the way they are.

Leave it. There are some relationships that are so toxic it would be in the best interests of everybody concerned, even the person who you feel is the main cause of the toxicity, that you leave that situation. In my experience in coaching a lot of people when they're in this type of relationship, what really makes matters worse for them is that on the one hand, they may feel that they must leave it, but on the other hand, they feel that they can't. It's that feeling of "I must leave, but I can't" that makes a person feel trapped, not in control of his life, and a victim. That is absolutely *not* having a life worth smiling about!

Now, I'm going to say something that is easier said than done, but it still doesn't invalidate the truth of the statement: if the first two options (change it or live with it) are not possible, then the *only other option* is to leave it—or stay miserable.

The bottom line for all of these techniques is that you have the power to create the life you want. Don't sit back and let it happen to you; proactively design the life you want, and let the smiles flow!

Smile Action Steps

* Think of one relationship that you currently are having a challenge with. What negative conclusions are you jumping to that may not be true?

_____

_____

_____

_____

_____

_____

_____

* If you were to take full responsibility for the challenge you are having in that relationship, what could you do? What action(s) could you take to turn that situation around?

_____

_____

_____

_____

_____

_____

CHAPTER 17

THE ATTITUDE OF GRATITUDE PHILOSOPHY: YOUR SECRET WEAPON

Life is like a camera. Just focus on what's important,
capture the good times, develop from the negatives,
and if things don't work out, take another shot.

—Author Unknown

There's an old expression that says that it takes money to make money. I also believe that success breeds more success. And, likewise, I believe that when you are more thankful for the things you have in your life—things like relationships, career, finances, possessions, and the like—your life will start to give you more reasons to be thankful.

The typical approach to life is that we think about what we *don't* have, then we set a goal to get what's missing. This method therefore focuses more on the things we don't have rather than what we do. But if there is some truth to the sayings that "it takes money to make money" and "success breeds more success," then it makes sense that by coming from a place of abundance, we will create more abundance in our life.

So, we should really be focusing more on an attitude of gratitude and appreciating the things that we *do* have in our lives. For instance, not too long ago, I got a puppy. She's a German Shepherd–hound mix. And in training her, I learned that the more I praised her for doing things correctly, the more she wanted to please me, because every time she pleases me by doing the correct thing, I give her a doggie treat. I think life is somewhat similar. The more you praise yourself and your life for the things you have and the things you have accomplished, the more life wants to give to you.

Appreciating What You Have

Do you know anybody who has the opposite of an attitude of gratitude? Such people always seem to be complaining about what they don't have or about other people, as if they were victims of their own lives. What's interesting about people of this type is that if they don't have something to complain about, they're almost certain to create a situation that gives them something to complain about. I love what Joyce Meyer says about worrying (this description holds especially true for complaining as well): "[Complaining] is like sitting in a rocking chair; you exert a lot of effort and energy, but you don't go anywhere."

It's impossible for you to complain about your life and have an attitude of gratitude at the same time. The more you focus on training your brain to look for all the positive aspects of what you do, the more your brain is going to look for more reasons to be happy about your life. And if you don't have those reasons, your brain will help you find them.

Some people are caught in the mentality of "this isn't it." This job that I have isn't it (there must be a better one out there); this relationship that I have isn't it (I can't wait to find someone better); this house that I bought isn't it. And so on and so on and so on. When a person has this endless loop of looking at his life, criticizing it, complaining about it, and saying, "This isn't it," even if he is given an opportunity that would increase the quality of his life, he wouldn't see it because his focus is on negative thoughts.

Let's do an experiment right now. Look around the room and pay attention to everything that is the color black. Go ahead, look around the room. Make a mental note of everything that is black, and when you're done, look back at this page. Now, while you're still reading this sentence and not taking your eyes off the book, I'd like you to name everything in the room that is the color red. Chances are that you missed everything that is red. Why? Because your focus was on everything that is black. If we focus on what's black in our lives, we're not going to see the bright colors that exist—the opportunities that will put a smile on our faces.

Have you ever gone on vacation to a place you've never been to before and you really wanted to soak up the city? You made sure that you saw the sights, took a lot of photos, ate at many different restaurants, and appreciated the scenery? One of my favorite trips was to Athens, Greece, and it blew me away. I love history. I love anything old. In fact, I collect antiques. I walked around these incredible monuments and temples that went back thousands of years. I visited the Stadium, where the first marathon ever was run. And as I was walking with my eyes and mouth wide open, just a bit like any traditional tourist, I thought to myself how lucky the local people were to live here. But do they take these spectacular sites for granted? Think about where you live. Do people come from out of town, even if it's not a major city, and get excited about being there? Do they walk around, take photos, and cherish the moment? What if we did that where we live? What if we walked around our neighborhoods and our house and the places that we take for granted on a day-by-day basis as if we were tourists and appreciated them? I'm sure we would all have much more gratitude for our lives.

When you come from a mental state of appreciating what you have, as you move forward in your life, the focus is no longer on trying to fill a void or fix something that you consider broken. When you're in the mental state of appreciating what you have, the goals and actions that you take are about creating the future, a powerful possibility.

This past Christmas, I was going through security at the airport, and there was this gentleman right behind me who, as he was gathering his stuff from the conveyor belt, was telling the TSA security person how excited he was to be seeing his 18-year-old daughter. He said that this was the first time that he was going to see her after 15 years. That's 15 years! Can you imagine? I mean, if you're a parent, you had not been able to see your child for 15 years, and you were just about to see her, how excited and happy would you be? How appreciative would you be? I couldn't help but ask him why it had taken 15 years for him to see his daughter. He explained to me that his ex-wife had left him 15 years ago and had taken his daughter with her. It was her mission to not let him see his daughter. Now, fortunately, he and his daughter had stayed in touch with e-mails and phone calls, but he had not been able to see her face-to-face. His daughter vowed that once she became of age and could make her own decisions legally, the first thing she would do was reach out to her father and see him for the holidays.

Now, I know some people who, if they were this man, would have spent the last 15 years angry that his ex had prevented him from having a relationship with his child. I don't know this particular gentleman, but after watching him for just a few minutes, I'm going to guess that for 15 years his focus was not on what he didn't have, but rather on his commitment to creating what he could have. In other words, he did not let the circumstances prevent him from having a powerful relationship with his daughter during those 15 years.

Let's look at your career. While I know that everything in your professional life may not be peachy keen, you can bring a sense of appreciation to your career. This would require a shift in focus from "what's missing" to "what's working." For instance, do you have a job? Does it pay you on a weekly or biweekly basis? Are you able to use what you earn to put food on the table for your family? Do you have opportunities to earn more if you achieve certain milestones? Do you like your coworkers? Any of these statements is a reason to have gratitude for your career. What other positive aspects of your working life can you think of? Remember, your job doesn't have to be perfect for you to appreciate it. The point is, *you're* responsible for your point of view. If showing gratitude for what you have helps you to create what you want, why not do it?

Suggestions for Building an Attitude of Gratitude

* *Wish yourself "happy birthday" each day.* I know this may sound a little silly. But let me share with you where the whole concept of singing "Happy Birthday" came from. In the past, there was a pagan belief that evil spirits would come whenever something good was about to happen in a person's life because these spirits wanted to mess it up. Celebrating a person's birthday was believed to help keep these negative spirits away. Some of your other evil spirits are actually your negative thoughts. So if each day when you wake up, the first thing you do is sing "Happy Birthday" to yourself, this small act might help keep those evil spirits that are living in your head away for the day.

* *Create a gratitude poster.* To help you focus on appreciating all the things that you have in your life, it might be a good idea for you to buy a flip chart from an office supply store and start to make a list of all the things that you are grateful for in your life—people, accomplishments, goals, or whatever brings positive meaning to you every day. Now, this is an exercise that you may not be able to do in one sitting, especially if you don't normally have an attitude of gratitude. So, I recommend that you take about 10 minutes, let it all flow out of your head onto this pad, and then keep the pad handy. As you think of other things to be grateful for, you can add them to your list. What will be interesting is that every time you see this pad, whether it's in your bedroom, your bathroom, or wherever, it'll be like the pad is asking you to focus on what you're grateful for and causing you to further seek out these things in your life.

* *Write a letter of gratitude to a special friend.* There may be a few people in your life who have made a big difference to

you. They may have given you some great advice when you
needed it, or they were there for you at all hours of the day
and night when you were going through a rough time. You
may want to write some nice long letters to tell them how
important they were to you during that time. It will make
you all feel wonderful and bring you closer together.

* *Make a call.* You may have some close friends or family
members who are very special to you, but whom you haven't
spoken to in a while. You may have been busy and simply
lost touch. Take 15 minutes and make one phone call a week
just to catch up with people who are important to you for
no other reason than to see how they're doing. You'll be glad
that you did.

Acknowledge Others

When you give appreciation to somebody for even the smallest thing,
it puts a smile on your face as well as his or hers. I believe that the best
acknowledgments are for people whom you just pass by and may never
encounter again. Trust me, it's well worth it.

Let me give you an example. I was in the Dallas airport, and I went
into the men's room. As I was washing my hands and drying them, I
noticed how incredibly clean and beautiful this particular bathroom
was. I mean, I've been in a lot of airport bathrooms, and this one stood
out. When I started to leave the bathroom, I noticed the janitor who
obviously was in charge of keeping this particular bathroom in top-
notch shape. So I decided to go over to him, and I said: "You know, I've
just got to tell you that I travel all over the world, and some months I'm
on the road more than I'm actually home. And because of the extensive
travel that I do, I see a lot of airport bathrooms, and this is the clean-
est and most beautiful bathroom I've ever had the pleasure of entering.

I wanted to thank you for doing such a great job because it makes my traveling life a little bit nicer when people have the level of commitment to excellence in their job the way you do. Thank you for what you do."

Let me ask you a question: How do you think that janitor felt after that acknowledgment? Did I put a smile on his face? *You betcha!* And do you think I felt good by making a difference with this gentleman? *Yes-siree!* It was as if it was Christmas, and we had just exchanged presents.

Here's the most powerful thing about this situation. Not only did he feel good and I feel good, but, more important, by my acknowledging him for a job well done, it enabled him to live from that commitment. In other words, as this gentleman goes through the rest of his day and perhaps the rest of his week or his month or his career, he may think back to that acknowledgment, feel empowered by it, and therefore want to hear more of it. So an acknowledgment like this can help transform a way of living for another person.

I'd like to take this opportunity to turn the tables on myself to show you the importance of acknowledgment. In my career as a professional trainer and motivator, I've had the privilege of working with students across the nation and around the world. One of my students recently paid me the utmost compliment. You see, Larry Gardner is a top producer in real estate. He's hardworking, successful, and many would say a model for his colleagues to emulate. But it wasn't always this way. In fact, Larry suffered through many setbacks in his life, some so severe that you wouldn't believe that we're talking about the same person here. Well, Larry and I sat down for lunch, and he confided in me about some of his past. He also told me how crucial my coaching and support have been for him, going so far as to say that I've played a key role in his personal transformation. I have to tell you, I was just so touched and pumped up after hearing his kind words.

Of course, I make a living doing what I do. I travel a lot, and I earn money and support my family through my career. But what Larry said to me was worth more to me than money. His acknowledgment made me want to work even harder to reach more people and make a difference in as many lives as I can.

Expect the Best

Many studies of high school students show how their self-perception is influenced by the external inputs that they face each day, and how this self-perception then dictates the way they act moving forward. For instance, if a high school student feels that he's not intelligent, even if it's not true, he will live based on that belief. If we tell a high school student that he's a stupid kid, that he needs extra help, or that he has challenges or is failing, that student is going to act based on those imposed beliefs. But if we acknowledge and reward him for his accomplishments and we focus more on those accomplishments than on the challenges that he might be having that empowers him to live based on this positivity and be more successful moving forward.

There was a study in which teachers were told that particular students had scored exceptionally high on standardized tests, and that they were considered gifted. The students were just average in their scores and had been chosen at random. Well, by the end of the year, the students that were labeled "gifted" had higher grades than their peers.[1]

So we see that positive acknowledgment is extraordinarily powerful in terms of enabling the people in our lives to live up to their potential. It also touches on the power of positive expectations. If you *expect* that someone will succeed—and treat him as if it was a rock-solid fact that he is already successful—he will be far more likely to succeed.

Smile Action Steps

* *"Make the Most of Your Time." 1,000 Marbles* by Jeffrey Davis is a great book that will give you some insight into how precious our time is and how important it is for us to spend it wisely, and with the people we love. After reading it, I followed the "marble" idea, and I've done it ever since. I'll explain the concept for you. I took a jar and bought a bunch of marbles. Then I picked a date and age in the future—in this case, my seventieth birthday—and I counted how many weeks I have between now and

then. (By the way, you can choose a different milestone date, if you like.) I then took the correct number of marbles based on those weeks and put them in the jar. Every week, when I come home from church on Sunday, I take out one of the marbles, hold it in my hand, and meditate for a minute or so, asking myself the question, "Did I live a life worth smiling about this week?" Was I a good father, a good provider, a good speaker, and a good business owner? Then I take that marble and throw it in the garbage, which reinforces for me the idea that I can never get that week back. This process reminds me that my years on this planet are finite, and that it's important that I stay focused on the things that truly add to the quality of my life.

* *Practice gratitude.* Right now, without delay, on a clean sheet of paper, or in the space given here, write down five things that you are grateful for in your life. Don't worry about the order that these come out in, and don't edit your thoughts. When you're done, fold up the paper and put it in your pocket, briefcase, or pocketbook or bookmark this page if you've written in the provided space here. Take it out several times a day to look at it, and by all means, add to it as something new occurs to you.

_____

_____

_____

_____

_____

_____

* *Practice acknowledgment.* Make it a new habit to acknowledge someone in your life every single day. It could be the clerk at the pharmacy, your child's teacher, the security guard in your office

building—anyone. Tell that person something positive about him- or herself, and watch how your words can make a positive impact. Who are a few people you can acknowledge in the next 24 hours?

_____

_____

_____

_____

_____

_____

_____

CONCLUSION

ike you, I have spent most of my life focusing on the question, "How does one go about being really happy?" How do we get to the place where we have a life worth smiling about? I'm sure you'd agree that we weren't born on this planet to live a life of struggle and frustration, worried about money, health, and relationships. In other words, I don't think we are supposed to be stressed out, freaked out, or zoned out most of our lives.

Although I've been doing seminars about this topic for years, it was only when I sat down to write this book on designing a life worth smiling about that I really started to analyze the subject fully. When you spend more than two years constantly asking questions, researching, investigating, and reading on just one topic, you learn quite a bit about it. I tried my best in this book to give you some of the tools and techniques that you can use to succeed in your personal and professional life, along with validating just how important smiling is for your well-being. I hope you found it useful and (dare I say it) fun!

There are a few points that I'd like to leave you with.

* *Don't forget what's really important.* In the pursuit of happiness, it's sometimes easy to think that money, career success, or material possessions reign supreme over all other facets of life. People without financial wealth wish that they had it, and of course those who already have it wish that they had more. But there are people who are the exception to that rule. Whether you have financial success or not, truly successful people are

those who realize that other people (friends and family) are what's truly important. They realize that when they are on their deathbed, they are not going to wish that they had saved more money or bought more things. When they get to the end of their lives, they will reflect, as we all will, on the quality of their life, and particularly on the relationships that they have had with others.

* *Constantly work to improve your attitude.* Though this has been said many times before, life truly is a journey, not a final destination. As you may have noticed, I like to use karate as an example. Please indulge me one more time. A martial arts master will tell you that being a black belt is not a final end result that you get to; rather, being a black belt is a place that you live from. You are always trying to deepen your mastery of the art. The idea is similar to owning and living in a house. When you live in a house, you have to continuously maintain it. Whether it's cutting the lawn, painting the siding, tweaking the decor, or moving furniture around, the house is never finished. In the same way, our lives are never "finished" while we're living; we are a work in progress, and we have to be committed to enjoying the journey. In order to best do this, be cognizant of your moods and your automatic thoughts. Strive to be open, upbeat, and committed to making a positive difference in your life and in the lives of those around you.

* *Improve 10 percent a month.* When we look at improving our entire life, it can be overwhelming, and taking on too much too quickly is a recipe for failure and frustration. If you take just one area of your life and improve in that area 10 percent a month, that's 120 percent a year (or more if you compound the results!). So take one area of your life (for example, health, relationships, money, or career goals) and apply the principles I covered in this book. Again, start with one area—and see what happens.

* *Don't forget to smile.* If there is one major aspect of this book that I hope has made a difference for you (and I certainly hope there is *more* than one), it's that no matter how you feel, smiling will make you feel better on both a physical and an emotional level. So no matter what may be going on in your life, don't forget to smile!

NOTES

Chapter 1

1. Ron Gutman, *Smile: The Astonishing Powers of a Simple Act* (New York: TED Books, 2011), Kindle Edition, p. 448.
2. Elaine N. Marieb and Katja Hoehn, *Human Anatomy & Physiology*, 9th ed. (Boston: Pearson, 2013), e-book, p. 599.
3. British Dental Health Foundation, "Yet Another Reason to Look After Your Teeth!," http://www.dentalhealth.org/news/details/209, accessed November 16, 2013.
4. Paul Ekman, Richard J. Davidson, and Wallace V. Friesen, "The Duchenne Smile: Emotional Expression and Brain Physiology II," *Journal of Personality and Social Psychology* 58, no. 2 (1990), pp. 342–353.
5. Tom Scheve, "How Many Muscles Does It Take to Smile?," *How Stuff Works*, http://science.howstuffworks.com/life/muscles-smile.htm, accessed November 16, 2013.
6. Sumathi Reddy, "Stress-Busting Smiles," *Wall Street Journal online*, February 25, 2013, http://online.wsj.com/news/articles/SB10001424127887323699704578326363601444362.
7. Fritz Strack, Leonard Martin, and Sabine Stepper, "Inhibiting and Facilitating Conditions of the Human Smile: A Nonobtrusive Test of the Facial Feedback Hypothesis," *Journal of Personality and Social Psychology* 54, no. 5 (1988), pp. 768–777.
8. Ibid.
9. Daniel Goleman, "A Feel-Good Theory: A Smile Affects Mood," *New York Times*, http://www.nytimes.com/1989/07/18/science/a-feel-good-theory-a-smile-affects-mood.html, accessed November 17, 2013.
10. Reddy, "Stress-Busting Smiles."
11. Goleman, "A Feel-Good Theory."
12. Daniel Goleman, "Long-Married Couples Do Look Alike, Study Finds," *New York Times*, http://www.nytimes.com/1987/08/11/science/long-married-couples-do-look-alike-study-finds.html, accessed November 17, 2013.
13. David T. Neal and Tanya L. Chartrand, "Embodied Emotion Perception: Amplifying and Dampening Facial Feedback Modulates Emotion Perception Accuracy," *Social Psychological and Personality Science* 2 no. 6 (2011), pp. 673–678.
14. Kimberly Gillan, "Botox Linked with Depression: Study," *Health Hub*, MSN New Zealand, http://health.msn.co.nz/healthnews/8642044/botox-linked-with-depression-study, accessed November 22, 2013.

15. "Cosmetic Injections Depression Link," BBC News, Health, http://www.bbc.co.uk/news/health-22106569, accessed November 22, 2013.

16. Alicia Sparks, "Face of Emotion: Dr. Eric Finzi on How Botox Affects Feelings, Moods," *PsychCentral*, http://blogs.psychcentral.com/celebrity/2013/03/face-of-emotion-dr-eric-finzi-on-how-botox-affects-feelings-moods/, accessed November 22, 2013.

17. R. B. Zajonc, "Feeling and Facial Efference: Implications of the Vascular Theory of Emotion," *Psychological Review* 96, no. 3 (1989), pp. 395–416.

18. Sarah Stevenson, "There's Magic in Your Smile: How Smiling Affects Your Brain," *Psychology Today online*, June 25, 2012, http://www.psychologytoday.com/blog/cutting-edge-leadership/201206/there-s-magic-in-your-smile.

19. Enid Burns, "Study Identifies Smiles as Form of Mimicry and Status," *RedOrbit*, October 15, 2012, http://www.redorbit.com/news/science/1112713369/smiles-mimicry-status-101512/.

20. Reddy, "Stress-Busting Smiles."

21. Manuel C. Voelkle, Natalie C. Ebner, Ulman Lindenberger, and Michaela Riediger, "Let Me Guess How Old You Are: Effects of Age, Gender, and Facial Expression on Perceptions of Age," *Psychology and Aging* 27, no. 2 (2012), pp. 265–277.

22. Stevenson, "There's Magic in Your Smile."

23. Ibid.

24. American Academy of Cosmetic Dentistry, "Whitening Survey, Spring 2011," http://www.aacd.com/proxy.php?filename=files/Footer%20Nav/Whitening%20Survey_Apr11.pdf, accessed November 24, 2013.

25. Anna Marie Mazoch, "Put On Your Happy Face," *Health & Medicine Blog*, *The Women's Journal*, October 1, 2013, http://thewomensjournal.com/2013/10/put-on-your-happy-face-2/.

26. Debra G. Walsh and Jay Hewitt, "Giving Men the Come-on: Effect of Eye Contact and Smiling in a Bar Environment," *Perceptual and Motor Skills* 61, no. 3, pt. 1, (1985), pp. 873–874, doi: 10.2466/pms.1985.61.3.873.

27. Jessica L. Tracy and Alec T. Beall, "Happy Guys Finish Last: The Impact of Emotion Expressions on Sexual Attraction," *Emotion* 11, no. 6 (2011), 1379–1387.

28. Marc Mehu, Karl Grammer, and Robin I. M. Dunbar, "Smiles When Sharing," *Evolution & Human Behavior* 28, no. 6 (2007), pp. 415–422.

29. "Researchers Measure the Value of a Smile," *Phys.org online*, May 10, 2011, http://phys.org/news/2011-05-researchers-measure-the-value-of.html.

30. Ryan T. Howell, "When You're Smiling (the Whole World Buys Your Toothpaste)," *Can't Buy Happiness Blog*, *Psychology Today*, August 12, 2012, http://www.psychologytoday.com/blog/cant-buy-happiness/201208/when-youre-smiling-the-whole-world-buys-your-toothpaste.

31. Laura P. Naumann, Simine Vazire, Peter J. Rentfrow, and Samuel D. Gosling, "Personality Judgments Based on Physical Appearance," *Personality and Social Psychology Bulletin* 35 (2009), p. 1661, originally published online September 17, 2009, doi: 10.1177/0146167209346309.

32. Serkan Toto, "Say Cheese: The Smile Scan Makes Grumpy Employees Friendlier," *TechCrunch*, January 30, 2009, http://techcrunch.com/2009/01/30/say-cheese-the-smile-scan-makes-grumpy-employees-friendlier/.

33. Kaima Negishi, "Smiling in the Post-Fordist 'Affective' Economy," *Transformations Journal*, no. 22, 2012, http://www.transformationsjournal.org/journal/issue_22/article_02.shtml.

34. Ernest L. Abel and Michael L. Kruger, "Smile Intensity in Photographs Predicts Longevity," *Psychological Science*, February 26, 2010, doi: 10.1177/0956797610 363775.

35. Lee Anne Harker and Dacher Keltner, "Expressions of Positive Emotion in Women's College Yearbook Pictures and Their Relationship to Personality and Life Outcomes Across Adulthood," *Journal of Personality and Social Psychology* 80, no. 1 (2001), pp. 112–124, http://www.psy.miami.edu/faculty/dmessinger/c_c/rsrcs/rdgs/emot/keltner_harker.yearbooksmiles.jpsp.pdf.

36. Paul Ekman, "Expression and the Nature of Emotion," reprinted online from K. Scherer and P. Ekman, *Approaches to Emotion* (Hillsdale, NJ: Lawrence Erlbaum, 1984), http://www.paulekman.com/wp-content/uploads/2013/07/Expression-And-The-Nature-Of-Emotion.pdf.

37. Daniel Lametti, "Can You Guess These Athletes' Nationalities?," *Slate online*, July 26, 2012, http://www.slate.com/articles/health_and_science/science/2012/07/olympic_smiles_how_to_identify_athletes_nationalities_based_on_their_facial_expressions_.html.

38. Lisa Collier Cool, "Surprising Facts About Smiling," *Yahoo! Health*, December 19, 2011, http://health.yahoo.net/experts/dayinhealth/science-smiles.

Chapter 4

1. Fred Rogers, "Senate Committee Hearing," *Fred Rogers Center—Advocacy for Children* exhibit video, 6:30, posted by "Fred Rogers Center" website, upload date unknown, http://exhibit.fredrogerscenter.org/advocacy-for-children/videos/view/969/.

2. Doreen Lorenzo, "Why Conviction Drives Innovation More than Creativity," *Fortune Tech, CNN Money*, October 17, 2011, http://tech.fortune.cnn.com/2011/10/17/innovation-creativity/.

Chapter 7

1. University College London, "How Long Does It Take to Form a Habit?," *UCL News*, August 4, 2009, http://www.ucl.ac.uk/news/news-articles/0908/09080401, accessed November 23, 2013.

2. Janet Rae-Dupree, "Can You Become a Creature of New Habits?," *New York Times*, May 4, 2008, http://www.nytimes.com/2008/05/04/business/04unbox.html?_r&_r=2&, accessed November 12, 2013.

3. Cathryn M. Delude, "Brain Researchers Explain Why Old Habits Die Hard," *MIT News*, October 19, 2005, http://web.mit.edu/newsoffice/2005/habit.html, accessed October 5, 2013.

4. Ibid.

5. Shawn Achor, *The Happiness Advantage: The Seven Principles of Positive Psychology That Fuel Success and Performance at Work* (New York: Crown Business, 2010), pp. 152–153.

Chapter 8

1. Stephen Covey, *The Seven Habits of Highly Successful People* (New York: Simon and Schuster, 1989), pp. 195–196.

Chapter 12

1. Madison Park, "Small Choices, Saved Lives: Near Misses of 9/11," *CNN*, September 5, 2011, http://www.cnn.com/2011/US/09/03/near.death.decisions/, accessed August 12, 2013.

Chapter 15

1. Kareem J. Johnson, Christian E. Waugh, Barbara L. Frederickson, "Smile to See the Forest: Facially Expressed Positive Emotions Broaden Cognition," *Psychology Press—Cognition and Emotion* 24, no. 2 (2010), pp. 299–321, doi: 10.1080/02699930903384667.

2. Jennipher Walters, "7 Good Reasons to Smile," *SparkPeople*, http://www .sparkpeople.com/resource/wellness_articles.asp?id=1529&page=3, accessed November 24, 2013.

3. "Researchers Measure the Value of a Smile," *Phys.org*, May 10, 2011, http://phys .org/news/2011-05-researchers-measure-the-value-of.html.

Chapter 17

1. Dr. Philip Zimbardo, "The Pygmalion Effect and the Power of Positive Expectations," YouTube video, 5:52, posted by "HeroicImagination TV," September 25, 2011, http://www.youtube.com/watch?v=hTghEXKNj7g.

INDEX

ABOUT THE AUTHOR

Darryl Davis began his career as an entertainer, appearing in movies and commercials. To help support himself while he pursued acting, he entered into real estate part-time at the age of 19. Eventually, he became a top-producing salesperson averaging six transactions per month. Later, he managed a sales organization that became the number one selling office in their market within its first six months of operation.

Darryl is now a renowned speaker, life coach, and creator of the nationally recognized term Next Level.® He is also the founder of the year-long coaching process The POWER Program®, which has proven results of doubling people's incomes over the previous year.

As a speaker, Darryl's contagious enthusiasm, hilarious sense of humor, depth of expertise, and flawless delivery are all jam-packed into a dynamic presentation of real world skills and techniques. He strives to bring his students to their Next Level® of success by training them on how to have more fun and less stress in their business and personal lives.

In addition to *How to Design a Life Worth Smiling About*, Darryl is the bestselling author of *How to Become a Power Agent in Real Estate* (McGraw-Hill, 2002) and *How to Make $100,000 a Year Your First Year in Real Estate* (McGraw-Hill, 2007).

For booking information, please visit www.DarrylSpeaks.com.

CPSIA information can be obtained
at www.ICGtesting.com
Printed in the USA
BVHW042302250119
538754BV00006B/23/P